Consciousness: A Very Short Introduction

VERY SHORT INTRODUCTIONS are for anyone wanting a stimulating and accessible way into a new subject. They are written by experts, and have been translated into more than 45 different languages.

The series began in 1995, and now covers a wide variety of topics in every discipline. The VSI library now contains over 500 volumes—a Very Short Introduction to everything from Psychology and Philosophy of Science to American History and Relativity—and continues to grow in every subject area.

Very Short Introductions available now:

ACCOUNTING Christopher Nobes
ADOLESCENCE Peter K. Smith
ADVERTISING Winston Fletcher
AFRICAN AMERICAN RELIGION
    Eddie S. Glaude Jr
AFRICAN HISTORY John Parker and
    Richard Rathbone
AFRICAN RELIGIONS
    Jacob K. Olupona
AGEING Nancy A. Pachana
AGNOSTICISM Robin Le Poidevin
AGRICULTURE Paul Brassley and
    Richard Soffe
ALEXANDER THE GREAT
    Hugh Bowden
ALGEBRA Peter M. Higgins
AMERICAN HISTORY Paul S. Boyer
AMERICAN IMMIGRATION
    David A. Gerber
AMERICAN LEGAL HISTORY
    G. Edward White
AMERICAN POLITICAL
    HISTORY Donald Critchlow
AMERICAN POLITICAL PARTIES
    AND ELECTIONS L. Sandy Maisel
AMERICAN POLITICS
    Richard M. Valelly
THE AMERICAN PRESIDENCY
    Charles O. Jones
THE AMERICAN REVOLUTION
    Robert J. Allison
AMERICAN SLAVERY
    Heather Andrea Williams
THE AMERICAN WEST Stephen Aron

AMERICAN WOMEN'S HISTORY
    Susan Ware
ANAESTHESIA Aidan O'Donnell
ANARCHISM Colin Ward
ANCIENT ASSYRIA Karen Radner
ANCIENT EGYPT Ian Shaw
ANCIENT EGYPTIAN ART AND
    ARCHITECTURE Christina Riggs
ANCIENT GREECE Paul Cartledge
THE ANCIENT NEAR EAST
    Amanda H. Podany
ANCIENT PHILOSOPHY Julia Annas
ANCIENT WARFARE
    Harry Sidebottom
ANGELS David Albert Jones
ANGLICANISM Mark Chapman
THE ANGLO-SAXON AGE John Blair
ANIMAL BEHAVIOUR
    Tristram D. Wyatt
THE ANIMAL KINGDOM
    Peter Holland
ANIMAL RIGHTS David DeGrazia
THE ANTARCTIC Klaus Dodds
ANTISEMITISM Steven Beller
ANXIETY Daniel Freeman and
    Jason Freeman
THE APOCRYPHAL GOSPELS
    Paul Foster
ARCHAEOLOGY Paul Bahn
ARCHITECTURE Andrew Ballantyne
ARISTOCRACY William Doyle
ARISTOTLE Jonathan Barnes
ART HISTORY Dana Arnold
ART THEORY Cynthia Freeland

Available soon:

For more information visit our website

www.oup.com/vsi/

Susan Blackmore

CONSCIOUSNESS

A Very Short Introduction

SECOND EDITION

OXFORD

UNIVERSITY PRESS

Great Clarendon Street, Oxford, OX2 6DP,
United Kingdom

Oxford University Press is a department of the University of Oxford.
It furthers the University's objective of excellence in research, scholarship,
and education by publishing worldwide. Oxford is a registered trade mark of
Oxford University Press in the UK and in certain other countries

First edition published 2005
Second edition published 2017

Published in the United States of America by Oxford University Press
198 Madison Avenue, New York, NY 10016, United States of America

British Library Cataloguing in Publication Data
Data available

Library of Congress Control Number: 2017938608

ISBN 978-0-19-879473-8

Printed and bound by
CPI Group (UK) Ltd, Croydon, CR0 4YY

Contents

List of illustrations

Chapter 1
Why the mystery?

The 'hard problem'

What is consciousness? This may sound like a simple question
but it is not. Consciousness is at once the most obvious and
the most difficult thing we can investigate. We seem either
to have to use consciousness to investigate itself, which is
a slightly weird idea, or to have to extricate ourselves from
the very thing we want to study. No wonder philosophers
have struggled for millennia with the concept; and for long
periods scientists refused even to study it. The good news is
that, in the 21st century, 'consciousness studies' is thriving.
Psychology, biology, and neuroscience have reached the point
where they are ready to confront some tricky questions:
What does consciousness do? Could we have evolved without
it? Is consciousness an illusion? What do we mean by
consciousness, anyway?

This does not mean that the mystery has gone away. Indeed, it is
as deep as ever. The difference now is that we know enough about
the brain to confront the problem head on. How on earth can the
electrical firing of millions of tiny brain cells produce this—my
private, subjective, conscious experience?

1. No one has yet succeeded in bridging the fathomless abyss, the great chasm, or the explanatory gap between inner and outer, mind and brain, or subjective and objective.

If we are going to get anywhere with understanding consciousness, we have to take this problem seriously, either by solving it or by showing why it is not really a problem at all. Some people claim to have solved the mystery of consciousness with grand, unifying theories, quantum physics, or spiritual theories involving mysterious powers of consciousness—but most simply ignore the yawning chasm, or 'fathomless abyss', between the physical and mental worlds (Figure 1). As long as they ignore this problem they are not really dealing with consciousness at all.

This problem is a modern incarnation of the famous mind–body problem with which philosophers have struggled for more than 2,000 years. The trouble is that in ordinary human experience there seem to be two entirely different kinds of thing, with no obvious way to bring them together.

On the one hand, there are our own experiences. Looking up from my work I can see trees, fields, and a bridge. I can hear the sound of the river and the buzzing of a fly. I can enjoy the warmth and familiarity of my own room, and wonder whether that scratching noise is the cat trying to get in. All of these are my own private experiences and they have a quality I cannot convey to anyone else. I may wonder whether your experience of green is the same as mine or whether coffee has exactly the same smell for you as it does for me, but I cannot find out. These ineffable (or indescribable) qualities are what philosophers call *qualia* (although there is much dispute about whether qualia exist or whether the concept is meaningful at all). The redness of that shiny red mug is a quale; the soft feel of my cat's fur is a quale; and so is that smell of coffee. These experiences seem to be real, vivid, and undeniable. They make up the world I live in. Indeed, they are all I have.

On the other hand, I really do believe that there exists a physical world out there that gives rise to these experiences. I may have doubts about what it is made of, or about its deeper nature, but I do not doubt that it exists. If I denied its existence I would not be able to explain why, if I go to the door, I shall probably find the cat there—and if you came by you would agree that there was now a cat trailing muddy footprints across my desk.

The trouble is that these two aspects of the world seem to be utterly different. There are real physical things, with size, shape, weight, and other attributes that we can measure and agree upon, and then there are private experiences—the feeling of pain, the colour of that apple as I see it now.

Throughout history most people have been *dualists*, believing in two different realms or worlds. This is also true of most non-Western cultures today with surveys suggesting it is true of most educated Westerners as well. This dualist belief begins early in life with children of 4 or 5 years old happily dividing the world into mental and physical things.

3

The major religions are almost all dualist, especially Christianity and Islam, which rely on the notion of an eternal, non-physical soul that can survive death and end up in heaven or hell. Many Hindus believe in the Atman or divine self, although the Advaita school advocates a non-dual philosophy that is becoming increasingly popular in the modern world. Non-duality is also found in the Buddhist concept of *anatta*, or no-self. The trouble is that it's hard to let go of the idea that 'I' and my private experiences are distinct from my body and brain.

Even among non-religious people, dualism is still prevalent. Popular New Age theories invoke the powers of mind, consciousness, or spirit, as though they were an independent force; and alternative therapists champion the effect of mind over matter, as though mind and body were two separate things. Such dualism is so deeply embedded in our language that we may happily refer to 'my brain' or 'my body'; as though 'I' am separate from 'them'.

In the 17th century the French philosopher René Descartes proposed the most famous dualist theory (Figure 2). Known as *Cartesian dualism*, this is the idea that mind and brain consist of different substances: the mind is non-physical and *non-extended* (i.e. it takes up no space); the body and the rest of the physical world are made of physical, or extended, substance. The trouble with this is obvious. How do the two interact? Descartes proposed that they meet in the tiny pineal gland in the centre of the brain, but this only staves off the problem a little. The pineal gland is a physical structure and Cartesian dualism provides no explanation of why it, alone, can communicate with the mental realm.

The interaction problem bedevils any attempt to build a workable dualist theory, which is probably why most philosophers and scientists completely reject dualism in favour of some kind of *monism* (the idea that there is only one kind of reality); but the

2. Descartes explained reflex responses to pain in terms of mechanical responses and the flow of 'animal spirits' in tiny tubes. But when it came to conscious experiences he proposed that they were part of a quite different mental world, connected to the physical body through the pineal gland in the centre of the brain.

options are few and problematic. Idealists make the mind fundamental but then must explain why and how there appears to be a consistent physical world. Neutral monists reject dualism but disagree about the fundamental nature of the world and how to unify it. A third option is *materialism* and this is by far the most popular among scientists today. Materialists take matter as fundamental, but then they face the problem that this book is all about—how to account for consciousness. How can a physical brain, made purely of material substances and nothing else, give rise to conscious experiences or ineffable qualia?

This problem is called the 'hard problem' of consciousness, a phrase coined in 1994 by the Australian philosopher David Chalmers. He wanted to distinguish this serious and overwhelming difficulty from what he called the 'easy problems'. The easy problems, according to Chalmers, are those that in principle we know how to solve, even if we have not yet done so. They include perception, learning, attention, and memory; how we discriminate objects or react to stimuli; how being asleep differs from being awake. All these are easy, he says, compared with the really hard problem of experience itself.

Not everyone agrees. Some claim that the hard problem does not exist; that it depends on a false conception of consciousness, or on drastically underestimating the 'easy' problems. The philosopher Massimo Pigliucci asks 'What hard problem?' calling it an illusion caused by 'the pseudo-profundity that often accompanies category mistakes'. And American philosopher Patricia Churchland calls it a 'hornswoggle problem', arguing that we cannot, in advance, decide which problems will turn out to be the really hard ones. It arises, she claims, from the false intuition that if we explained perception, memory, attention, and all the other details, there would still be something left out—'consciousness itself'.

These are important objections. So before we go any further we must delve into what, if anything, 'consciousness itself' might mean.

Defining consciousness

What is it like to be a bat? This curious question looms large in the history of consciousness studies. First asked in the 1950s, it was made famous by the American philosopher Thomas Nagel in 1974. He used the question to challenge materialism, to explore what we mean by consciousness, and to see why it makes the mind–body problem so intractable. What we mean, he said, is *subjectivity*. If there is something it is like to be the bat—something *for the bat*

Box 1 Defining consciousness

There is no generally agreed definition of consciousness, but the following are ways often used to talk about it.

'What it's like to be...': If there is something it is like to be for an animal (or computer; or baby) then that animal (or computer; or baby) is conscious. Otherwise it is not.

Subjectivity or *phenomenality*: Consciousness means subjective experience or phenomenal experience. This is the way things seem to me, as opposed to how they are objectively.

Qualia (singular: *quale*, pronounced qua-lay): The ineffable subjective qualities of experience, such as the redness of red or the indescribable smell of turpentine. Some philosophers claim that qualia do not exist.

The hard problem: How do subjective experiences arise from objective brains?

itself—then the bat is conscious. If there is nothing it is like to be the bat, then it is not (Box 1).

So think, for example, of the mug, mouse mat, or book on your table. Now ask yourself—what is it like to be the mug? You will probably answer that it is like nothing at all; that mugs cannot feel, that china is inert, and so on. You will probably have no trouble in opining that mugs and mats are not conscious. But move on to worms, flies, bacteria, or bats and you may have more trouble. You do not know, and have no idea how to find out, what it is like to be an earthworm. Even so, as Nagel points out, if you think that there is something it is like to be the worm, then you believe that the worm is conscious.

Nagel chose the bat as his example because bats are so very different from us. They fly in the dark, hang upside-down from trees or in damp caves, and use sonar as well as vision. They emit rapid bursts of high-pitched squeaks while they fly and then, by analysing the echoes that come back to their sensitive ears, learn about the world around them.

What is it like to experience the world this way? It is no good imagining that you are a bat because an educated, speaking bat would not be a normal bat at all; conversely, if *you* became a normal bat and could not think or speak then you would not be able to answer your own question.

Nagel argued that we can never know the answer to this question and he concluded that the problem is insoluble. For this reason he is dubbed a *mysterian*. Another mysterian is the American philosopher Colin McGinn, who argues that we humans are 'cognitively closed' with respect to consciousness. That is, we have no hope of understanding it, just as a dog has no hope of being able to read the newspaper he so happily carries back from the shops. Psychologist Stephen Pinker agrees: we may be able to understand most of the detail of how the mind works, yet consciousness itself may remain forever beyond our reach.

Not many people share Nagel's pessimism, but his question has proved helpful in reminding us what is at stake when we talk about consciousness. It is no good learning about perception, memory, intelligence, or problem-solving as purely physical processes and then claiming to have explained consciousness. If you are really talking about consciousness, then you must deal with subjectivity. Either you must actually solve the hard problem and explain how subjectivity arises from the material world or, if you claim that consciousness is an illusion or even that it does not exist at all, you must explain why it *appears* so strongly to exist.

Subjective experience or 'what it's like to be...' is also called *phenomenality*, or *phenomenal consciousness*, terms coined by

American philosopher Ned Block. He divides phenomenal consciousness (what it is like to be in a certain state) from *access consciousness* (availability for use in thinking or guiding action and speech). Others deny there is any difference, but phenomenal consciousness (or phenomenality, or subjectivity) is what Nagel was talking about and is the core of the problem of consciousness.

With these ideas in mind, we are ready to face a fundamental divide in consciousness studies. This concerns the following question: Is consciousness an extra ingredient added to our ability to perceive, think, and feel, or is it inseparable from being able to perceive, think and feel? To put it another way, are qualia or subjective experiences something in addition to being a living, thinking, feeling creature? This really is the key question on which the rest depends, and you might like to decide now on your own answer, for the implications either way are quite striking.

On the one hand, if consciousness is an extra added ingredient then we naturally want to ask why we have it, what it's for, what it does, and how we got it. We might imagine that we could have evolved without it, and so we want to know why we have this added extra, what advantages it gave us, and whether it evolved in other creatures too. This means that the hard problem is indeed hard; and the task ahead is to answer these difficult questions.

On the other hand, consciousness might be intrinsic to complex biological processes and inseparable from them. This is the view in both materialism (everything in the universe is matter) and functionalism (any animal or machine that carried out the appropriate functions would necessarily be conscious too). In this case there is no need to ask why consciousness evolved, because any creature that evolved with intelligence, perception, memory, and emotions would necessarily be conscious as well. There is no added extra and no sense in talking about 'consciousness itself' or 'ineffable qualia'. Thinking about consciousness this way, there is no deep mystery, and no hard problem. What we need to do is explain why there *seems* to be a hard problem and why we *seem* to be having ineffable, non-physical, conscious experiences. In other words, consciousness is an illusion because neither consciousness nor the hard problem are what they seem to be. So the task is to explain how the illusions come about.

If the implications of this dichotomy seem hard to grasp, a thought experiment might help.

Zombie

Imagine someone who looks like you, acts like you, and speaks like you, but who is not conscious at all. This outwardly identical other you has no inner world, no conscious experiences, and no qualia; all its actions are carried out 'in the dark' without the light of awareness. This unconscious creature—not some half-alive Haitian corpse—is the 'philosophical zombie'.

Zombies are easy to imagine, but could they exist? This apparently simple question leads to a world of philosophical difficulties because if zombies can exist then physicalism is false and some kind of dualism has to be true.

On the 'yes' side are those who believe it possible to have two apparently identical systems; one conscious, the other unconscious. Chalmers says 'yes', claiming that zombies are not only imaginable but possible—in some other world if not in this one. He imagines his zombie twin who behaves exactly like the real Chalmers but has no conscious experiences, no inner world, and no qualia. All is dark inside the mind of zombie-Dave. Other philosophers have dreamed up thought experiments involving a zombie Earth populated by zombie people, or speculated that some real live philosophers might actually be zombies pretending to be conscious.

On the 'no' side are those who believe the whole idea of zombies is absurd, including both Churchland and American philosopher

Daniel Dennett. The idea is ridiculous, they claim, because any system that could walk, talk, think, play games, choose what to wear, or enjoy a good dinner would necessarily be conscious. When people imagine a zombie they cheat by not taking the definition seriously enough. So if you don't want to cheat, remember that the zombie has to be completely indistinguishable from a normal person. It won't help to ask the zombie questions about its experiences or philosophy, because *by definition* it must behave just as a conscious person would. If you really follow the rules, the critics say, the idea disappears into nonsense (Figure 3).

It should now be easy to see that the zombie is a vivid way of thinking about the key question: Is consciousness an added extra that we conscious humans are lucky to have, or does it necessarily come along with all our evolved skills of perceiving, thinking, and feeling? If you believe that it's an added extra, then we could all have evolved as zombies instead of as conscious people and you may be tempted to ask why we did not. You might even start

3. **The idea of the philosopher's zombie leads only to confusion.**

wondering whether your best friend is a zombie. But if you believe that consciousness is inseparable from the skills we humans have, then zombies could not exist and the whole idea is daft.

I think the whole idea is daft. Nevertheless, it remains extremely alluring, largely because it is so easy to imagine a zombie. Yet being easy to imagine something is not a good guide to the truth. So let's consider another aspect of the same problem—whether consciousness does anything.

The phrase 'the power of consciousness' is common in popular discourse. The idea is that consciousness is some sort of force that can directly influence the world—either by acting on our own bodies, as when 'I' consciously decide to move my arm and it moves—or, more controversially, in things like psychic healing, telepathy, or 'mind over matter'. Like the zombie, this 'power' is easy to imagine. We can visualize our conscious mind controlling our bodies and influencing things. But does this idea make any sense? As soon as you remember that consciousness means subjectivity or phenomenality, then the idea seems less plausible. How could 'what it's like to be' something act as a force or power? How could my *experience* of the green of that tree cause something to happen?

One way to explore this idea is to ask what would happen if you took someone's consciousness away. Obviously, if consciousness has any power at all, what would be left could not be a zombie because the zombie must, by definition, be indistinguishable from a conscious person. So you would be left with someone who was different from a conscious person because...what?

Perhaps you think we need consciousness to make decisions, but neuroscience shows us how the brain makes decisions and it does not seem to need an extra, added force to do so. Artificial systems are making increasingly complex decisions without needing a consciousness module. The same goes for seeing, hearing, controlling action, and many other human abilities. The more we learn about the brain the less room there is for consciousness to play a role. Perhaps you think it is needed for aesthetic appreciation, creativity, or falling in love, but, if so, you would have to show that these things are done by consciousness itself rather than by the workings of a clever body and brain.

All this leads to the awkward notion that perhaps consciousness does nothing, and other oddities point the same way. For example, think about people catching cricket balls, playing table tennis, or interrupting fast-flowing conversations. These quick actions may seem to be done consciously, but is it the consciousness itself that makes them happen? In fact, as we shall see, such actions happen too fast. Could consciousness, then, be completely powerless? One version of this idea is *epiphenomenalism*—the idea that consciousness is a useless by-product or *epiphenomenon*. But this is a very curious notion because it entails consciousness actually existing but having no effects on anything else. And if it has no effects it is hard to see how we could end up worrying so much about it—or even talking about it.

But epiphenomenalism is not the only way of understanding consciousness as being powerless. An alternative is that any creature that can see, feel, think, fall in love, and appreciate a fine wine will inevitably end up believing they are conscious, imagining zombies are possible, and thinking that consciousness does things. The bottom line for this kind of theory is that we are deluded; we feel as though our consciousness is a power or added ability and so we believe it is, but we are wrong. If this theory needs a name, we might call it 'delusionism'.

I think this is the right way to think about consciousness, but it implies that our ordinary assumptions about our own minds are deeply misguided. Could we really be so wrong? And if so, why? Perhaps we should take a closer look at some of those everyday assumptions.

The theatre of the mind

The most natural way to think about consciousness is probably something like this. The mind is like a private theatre inside my head, where I sit looking out through my eyes. But this is a multi-sensational theatre with touches, smells, sounds, and emotions. And I can use my imagination to conjure up sights and sounds as though seen on a mental screen or heard by my inner ear. All these thoughts and impressions are the 'contents of my consciousness' and 'I' am the audience of one who experiences them (Figure 4).

This theatre imagery fits happily with another common image of consciousness—that it flows like a river or stream. In the 19th century, the 'father of modern psychology', William James, coined the phrase 'the stream of consciousness' and it seems apt enough. Our conscious life really does feel like a flowing stream of sights, sounds, smells, touches, thoughts, emotions, worries, and joys—all of which happen, one after another, to me.

This way of conceiving of our own minds is so easy, so natural, that it hardly seems worth questioning. Yet when we get into an intellectual muddle, as we have with the problem of consciousness, it may be worth challenging some basic assumptions—in this case, these apparently innocent analogies.

The strongest challenge comes from Dennett who argues that while most people are happy to reject Cartesian dualism, they still retain dualist thinking in imagining what he calls the *Cartesian theatre*. This is not just the analogy of the mind with a theatre, but the notion that somewhere in the mind or brain there must be a place and time at which everything comes together and 'consciousness happens'; or a finishing line in the brain's activities, after which things mysteriously become conscious or 'enter consciousness'.

This has to be false, claims Dennett, because the brain is a parallel, distributed processing system with no central headquarters and no place in which 'I' could sit, making decisions and watching the show as things pass through my consciousness. Instead, the many different parts and processes of the brain just get on with their own jobs, communicating with each other when necessary, and with no central control. What, then, could correspond to the theatre of consciousness? Somehow we have to understand how this feeling of being a conscious self who is having a stream of experiences comes about in a brain that really has no inner theatre, no show, and no audience.

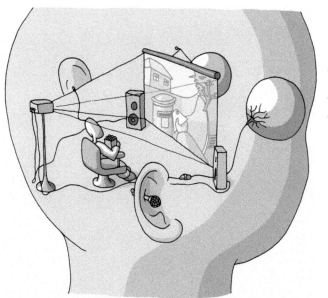

4. I feel as though I am somewhere inside my head looking out—that I experience the outside world through my eyes and ears; imagine things in my mind's eye; and direct my arms and legs to walk me down the street and post the letter. But there is no place inside the brain where I could be. This is Dennett's mythical Cartesian theatre.

Dennett coined the term 'Cartesian materialist' to describe people who claim to reject dualism but still believe in the Cartesian theatre. Few admit to being one. Yet ideas such as the stream of consciousness and the theatre of the mind remain as popular as ever. They may, of course, be right, and if so the task of a science of consciousness is to explain what that metaphorical theatre corresponds to in the brain and how it works. But I rather doubt they are. Exploring a little more about how the brain works may help us to see why.

Chapter 2
The human brain

A big brain

Said to be the most complex object in the known universe, a human brain, at nearly 1.5 kg or 3 lbs, is about three times larger than it should be by comparison with our closest relatives, the other great apes. It contains about 100 billion *neurons* (i.e. nerve cells) connected by trillions of synapses, as well as billions of supporting glial cells and blood vessels. The brain and spinal cord together make up the central nervous system, the spinal cord being connected to the brain stem and then midbrain which is responsible, among other things, for controlling the sleep–wake cycle. Behind this lies the *cerebellum*, or 'little brain', mostly concerned with fine movement control, and above it is the latest part of the brain to evolve, the *cerebral cortex* (i.e. the outer layer of the brain). This is the part that shows the greatest differences from other species and is divided into four lobes, occipital at the back, temporal above the ears, parietal at the top, and frontal, of course, at the front.

Although long-range connections and networks run throughout the brain, specific areas have distinct functions. The *somatosensory cortex* at the top of the brain deals with touch, and stimulating any part of it causes a sensation as though the corresponding part of the body is being touched. Close by is the *motor cortex* and if this is stimulated a part of the body moves. Nearly a quarter of the human brain, largely the *occipital lobe*, is taken up with processing visual information whether this comes in through the eyes or is evoked in imagination, memory, and dreaming. The *auditory cortex* deals with hearing, and deep down inside the brain is the *limbic system* concerned with instinctive responses and basic emotions including fear, hunger, and sexual arousal. The *frontal lobe* involves many complex functions including attention, planning, and decision-making, self-control, and motivation. Memory functions are widely distributed but the *hippocampus* in the limbic system is essential for laying down new memories and the *temporal lobe* for storing and retrieving them.

Much of this knowledge was obtained from studying the effects of brain damage, stimulating the brain with electrodes, or recording from it using EEG (electroencephalogram), but new methods of brain scanning can reveal what is happening deep inside the brain. It is even becoming possible to tell, from brain activity, what someone is seeing or thinking about. In one method, scientists record many hours of scan data while subjects watch videos. From this a huge 'dictionary' is created that relates the shapes, edges, and movements in the videos to neural activity at several thousand points in the viewer's brain. When that same person watches a new video, their dictionary can be used to reconstruct what was seen. The computational power required is vast and early reconstructions were hazy but they were recognizable as scenes in the video and are getting better all the time.

But where does consciousness fit in? In some ways, the better we understand the brain, the more mysterious consciousness becomes. We cannot deny that the brain is intimately involved in consciousness because drugs that affect brain function affect subjective experience; stimulation induces specific hallucinations, physical sensations, or emotional reactions; and damage to the brain can drastically affect a person's state of consciousness. Yet the brain does not seem designed to produce the kind of consciousness we have. Most characteristically the brain is a massively parallel and distributed system with no central organization, no inner sanctum where the really important bits happen. A brain is more like a vast network—or a vast collection of interpenetrating networks—than a personal computer with a central processor.

By contrast, human consciousness seems to be unified—but why and how?

The unity of consciousness

This *unity of consciousness* is often described in three ways, all of which are implied when consciousness is likened to a theatre or a stream of experiences.

First, there is the unity of those things I am experiencing in the 'now'—that is, at any time some things are in my consciousness while many others are not. Those inside are called the *contents of consciousness*: the experiences in the stream or the show on the stage of the theatre. Second, consciousness seems unified over time in that there seems to be continuity from one moment to the next, or even across a whole lifetime. Third, these conscious contents are experienced by the same 'me'. In other words, there is a single and continuing experiencer.

A successful science of consciousness must therefore explain the contents of consciousness, the continuity of consciousness, and the self who is conscious, and it must do so starting with a massively parallel and non-centralized brain. We'll return to the question of self, but for now let's begin with the apparently innocent idea that there are contents of consciousness.

The important point here is that most of what goes on in the brain seems to be outside of consciousness and even inaccessible to consciousness. We see the trees blowing in the wind, but we are not conscious of all the rapid electrical activity in the visual cortex that leads up to that perception. We consciously reply to an email, but we are unconscious of how our hands type the words or where the words are coming from. We consciously struggle to win a game of table tennis, oblivious to the fast visuo-motor control that makes our winning shots possible.

In all these cases every one of our brain's cells, with their billions of connections, is active—some firing faster and some slower, depending on what we are doing. Yet most of this activity never makes it into the stream of consciousness or the theatre of my mind. So we call it unconscious or subconscious, or we relegate it to the fringe of consciousness.

But what does this really mean? The problem is that this distinction implies a kind of magical difference between the conscious bits and the unconscious bits. Is conscious brain activity controlled by a supernatural soul or non-physical self, as a dualist might believe? Is there a special place in the brain where consciousness happens? Are there special types of 'consciousness neuron' that produce conscious experiences while all the rest do not? Are there certain ways of connecting up neurons that produce consciousness? Or what? As we shall see, there are theories of consciousness corresponding to all these possibilities, but all face severe difficulties.

In the end, the question seems to be this—do we struggle on with the familiar view of consciousness as a theatre or stream of experiences and try to make it work, or do we throw out all our familiar ways of thinking and begin again? It is worth bearing this question in mind as we consider some of the fascinating research that links consciousness to brain function (Box 2).

The neural correlates of consciousness

Everyone has experienced pain. Pain is horrid. It hurts and we don't like it. But what is it? Pain is a perfect example for considering the

Box 2 Synaesthesia

Some people hear shapes, see noises, or feel sounds, and this odd form of unified consciousness is surprisingly common. Many young children have *synaesthesia* but the effects usually disappear with age, leaving something like one in 200 adults as synaesthetes. Synaesthesia runs in families, is more common in women and left-handers, and is associated with good memory but poorer maths and spatial ability. It is especially prevalent among poets, writers, and artists.

In the most common form of synaesthesia, numbers or letters are always seen as coloured. These experiences cannot be consciously suppressed, and when tested after many years most synaesthetes report that exactly the same shapes or forms or colours are induced by the same stimuli. Many synaesthetes hide their abilities, and for a long time psychologists doubted they were real, but recent research has confirmed the prevalence and stability of the effects.

Synaesthetes may have more connections between the different sensory areas of the brain, and Ramachandran argues that since numbers and colour are processed in adjacent areas this might explain the most common form of synaesthesia.

neural correlates of consciousness (NCC); that is, the brain events that are correlated, or associated, with subjective experiences.

On the subjective side, pain is a private experience that we cannot describe to anyone else. We cannot know how bad someone else's pain is, except by watching their behaviour, and even then we might think that they are bluffing when they cry. We cannot even remember how pain feels once it is gone. Perhaps the only way we can really know what pain is like is when we are suffering it right now.

On the objective side, when pain is caused by injury chemical changes take place at the injured site and signals pass along specialized neurons called *C-fibres* to the spinal cord, and from there to the brain stem, thalamus, somatosensory cortex (which includes a map of the body), and cingulate cortex. Brain scans show a strong correlation between the amount of pain experienced and the amount of activity in these areas. In other words, we know some of the neural correlates of pain.

Yet it is important to remember that 'correlation does not imply cause'. For example, suppose that Freddie has a habit of going into the living room and turning on the television. Almost every time he does so, his action is soon followed by the Simpsons coming on. If this correlation implied cause then we would conclude that Freddie's action caused the Simpsons to appear. In this case, of course, we are not fooled. But in many other cases we might be.

The rule of thumb to remember is this: Whenever there is a reliable correlation between A and B there are three possible causal explanations: A caused B, B caused A, or A and B were both caused by something else. In addition, A and B might actually be the same thing even though they do not appear to be so (like water and H_2O; or the morning and evening stars).

Which is the case with pain? Maybe the physical changes *cause* the pain, in which case we have to solve the hard problem. Maybe the pain causes the physical changes, in which case we need a supernatural theory. Maybe something else causes both but we have no idea what. Or maybe they are really the same thing. Many materialists argue for this last explanation, but if it is true we have absolutely no idea how it could be true. How could this awful, toe-curling, horrible, unwanted feeling in the side of my head actually *be* the firing of my C-fibres?

This question illustrates the depth of our present ignorance about consciousness, but we should not despair. Science has a habit of solving what seem to be impossible problems and may do so again. Francis Crick, Nobel prize-winner and co-discoverer of the structure of DNA, argued for tackling the problem of consciousness the same way as science often does—by starting with correlations before trying to discover causes—and so the hunt for the NCCs began, defined by his colleague Christof Koch as 'the minimum neural mechanisms sufficient for any one specific conscious percept'.

Look at the Necker cube in Figure 5. You cannot help seeing this in depth and the cube will flip between two different interpretations; you may even be able to flip it deliberately. It feels as though first one view comes into consciousness and then the other; as though the two views are competing for consciousness. In *binocular rivalry* the same flipping can be induced by showing different images to each eye. Again the two are not fused but awareness flips between the two. This provides an ideal opportunity to study the neural correlates of particular

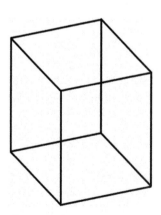

5. This ambiguous figure is called a Necker cube. If you keep looking at it for some time you will find that it flips between two equally possible interpretations, as though the two views are competing for consciousness. But is this the right way of thinking about what is happening?

experiences, or 'specific conscious percepts' because the image on the retina stays the same while the experience flips. If we could find out which parts of the brain stay the same and which flip when the experience flips, this might mean that we had found the place where the perceptions 'enter consciousness', or located the centre of visual awareness—or even identified 'consciousness neurons'.

Monkeys apparently experience the same flipping as we do and can press a lever to say which percept they are currently seeing. So in the 1980s, the Greek biologist Nikos Logothetis inserted electrodes in different parts of monkey brains, including the primary visual cortex (V1), later visual areas (V4), and temporal cortex where some visual information goes after initial processing. The results showed that neural activity in V1 stayed the same all the time, but activity in higher areas changed when the monkey's experience changed.

For some researchers this implied that the NCCs had been located. Indeed Crick himself concluded that we are not conscious of processing in early sensory areas but only of the later results of that processing. But this conclusion may have been too hasty. When similar experiments became possible using human subjects in brain scanners, broadly similar results were obtained with activity in higher visual areas more often changing when the perception changed, but such changes have also been found in V1 and even in earlier visual areas before the information reaches V1. And the fundamental problem remains. We still have no idea what it means to say that consciousness 'arises' or is 'generated' in one brain area rather than another. When we have found brain cells that change with changes in conscious perception, we must still ask—How? Why? What is the 'magic difference'? How can some cells give rise to subjective experiences and some not?

There are other more practical objections, including the worry that the findings might reflect the precursors or consequences of consciousness rather than 'consciousness itself'. When monkeys press a lever or people say, 'Now I see the face', the brain activity measured might be a correlate of reporting what was seen rather than of the experience itself. To test this, scientists have used varieties of *contrastive analysis* to compare conscious with unconscious experiences, as well as 'no-report' methods such as watching pupil dilation and other indicators of the flipping perception. These studies show that when the correlates of reporting are removed many of the differences disappear.

Where do we go from here? Some will say that we are closing in on the NCCs and will soon identify consciousness neurons or pin down the specific process that creates qualia or bridges the gulf between the brain and consciousness. From there, they might say, it is a small step to solving the hard problem. An alternative is that the whole enterprise is misconceived—that what we will find, with increasing detail and certainty, is the neural correlates of specific perceptions, thoughts, and decisions but never of 'consciousness itself', for there is no such thing. In this case the task is to explain why there seems to be such a thing.

Damaged minds

A stroke occurs when arteries are blocked or blood vessels in the brain burst and bleed into the brain. Either way the brain cells are deprived of oxygen and are damaged. This frequently causes paralysis, blindness, and other deficits on the opposite side of the body. This makes sense because the left brain controls the right side of the body and the left brain sees the right side of the visual world (that is, it deals not with the right eye, but with everything that is seen to the right of centre). A much odder effect sometimes follows a stroke in the right parietal lobe.

In unilateral, hemispatial, or hemifield neglect patients don't just lose specific abilities; rather they seem to lose half their world. It is not just that they cannot see when they look towards the left side of a room, or the left side of a picture, but rather that they seem not to realize that there even is a left side. This becomes obvious through their odd behaviour. For example, they might eat only the food on the right side of their plate and completely ignore the rest until someone else turns the plate round. They might shave only the right side of their face, or respond only to visitors who stand on the right. Asked to draw familiar objects they draw only the right side and even in dreams most of their eye movements are to the right (Figure 6).

The Italian neurologist Edoardo Bisiach carried out a unique experiment asking such patients to imagine the famous cathedral

6. These drawings were made by patient PP who suffered a right hemisphere stroke in 1987. Note how much is missing from the left hand side of each one. She continued to show signs of visual neglect until her death seventeen years later.

square in Milan, which they all knew well. First, they had to describe what they would see if they were arriving at the Duomo from the north side. They all described the many beautiful buildings, shops, and cafés that they would see to their right and ignored everything that would be to their left if they were standing there. Next he invited them to imagine coming into the square from the opposite side. Now all the forgotten buildings were carefully described and the previously remembered ones forgotten.

What is going on? It is very difficult to accept that human experience could be fragmented like this. We like to imagine that surely if we had a stroke we would be able to recognize our silly mistake and bring the two views together, but clearly this just does not happen. For these people, half the world is simply gone and there is no higher conscious self who can overcome the problem.

Memory is also something we can easily take for granted until we consider the effects of losing it. There are two main types of memory, short and long term, but this major distinction can hide the many varied and subtle kinds of memory associated with specific tasks and abilities. This is important in older people whose memory for events is fading but who may still come to recognize places and routines, and learn new motor skills. Also, small areas of brain damage can affect very specific kinds of memory.

The most dramatic loss, and the most interesting for thinking about consciousness, is *anterograde amnesia*. This occurs when the hippocampus (part of the brain's limbic system) is damaged, whether from Korsakoff's syndrome caused by alcohol poisoning, or from surgery, illness, or accidents that deprive the brain of oxygen. The result is that the person retains their short-term memory and the long-term memories they already have, but cannot lay down new long-term memories. So the rest of their life occurs as an ever-rolling present of a few seconds, which then disappears into blankness.

HM was one of the most famous cases of amnesia ever studied. He had both hippocampi removed in 1956 in a last-ditch attempt to control severe epilepsy, and was left profoundly amnesic. He could learn some new skills and became quicker at recognizing certain stimuli, but he always denied ever having done the tasks or seen the stimuli before. CW was a musician who lost his memory through encephalitis. After the illness he could still enjoy music, sight-read, and even conduct his choir, but he could not remember the rehearsals or any other events that happened from then on.

Neurologist Oliver Sacks describes his experience with Jimmie G., a victim of Korsakoff's syndrome who, at the age of 49, still believed he was 19 and had just left the navy. Out of curiosity, Sacks showed Jimmie his own reflection in a mirror, but quickly regretted his action when Jimmie saw his own now grey-haired face and became frantic with fear and incomprehension. So Sacks quickly led him over to the window where he noticed some kids playing outside. Jimmie's fear subsided, he began to smile, and Sacks stole guiltily away. When he returned Jimmie greeted him as though he were a stranger.

In his diary, CW wrote the same words again and again: 'I have just become conscious for the first time'. Others exclaim, over and over, 'I have just woken up'. Perhaps we all know that vivid feeling of suddenly becoming acutely conscious, as though we had been dreaming or submerged in thought. This may be triggered by the beauty of our surroundings, by a chance word or comment, or even by asking ourselves the question, 'Am I conscious now?', and can be a strange and special moment. But imagine living life in a perpetual process of awakening that you can never remember.

What is it like to be so deeply amnesic? Are HM and CW fully conscious? Are they conscious in a different way? Do they experience their consciousness as continuous in the way most of us do? If we could detect consciousness, measure it, or even define it properly, then we might get answers, but we cannot. While these amnesics are obviously awake, alert, interested in the world, and can describe how they feel, they cannot have any sense of yesterday turning into today, or of planning for a future that connects to their past.

If you believe in any kind of inner self, soul, or spirit, these facts are awkward to face. Is there a real self somewhere who is remembering everything but just cannot convey it to the damaged brain? Has the soul or self been damaged too, exactly in line with the physical damage? More likely is that our sense of being a continuous, conscious self is somehow manufactured by a fully functioning brain, but how? Some even odder kinds of brain damage challenge the very idea of the unity of consciousness.

Seeing without seeing

DF is a patient with visual form *agnosia*. Even though her basic visual ability and her colour vision are normal, she cannot recognize the forms or shapes of objects by sight, name simple line drawings, or recognize letters and digits. She can, however, reach out and grasp everyday objects with remarkable accuracy, even though she cannot say what they are.

In a fascinating experiment, DF was shown a series of slots—like those you might post a letter through—and asked to draw the orientation of the slot, or to adjust a line to the angle of the slot. She could not do this at all. However, when she was given a piece of card she could quickly line it up with the slot and post it through.

At first sight this might look as though DF is able to see (because she can post the cards) without having the *actual experience* of seeing; it would imply a dissociation between vision and consciousness, as though she were a visual zombie. This conclusion follows from our natural way of thinking about vision and consciousness, but research suggests that this conclusion is wrong.

The most natural way of thinking about vision is probably something like this: information comes into the eyes and is processed by the brain; this leads to our consciously seeing a picture of the world which we can then act upon. In other words, we must consciously see something before we can act on it. It turns out that the brain is not organized this way at all, and we could probably not survive if it were. In fact, there are (at least) two distinct visual streams with different functions (Figure 7).

The *ventral stream* leads from V1 forward into the temporal cortex and is involved in recognizing objects and perceiving the world. But this takes time. So, in parallel with this, the *dorsal stream* leads into the parietal lobe and contributes to fast

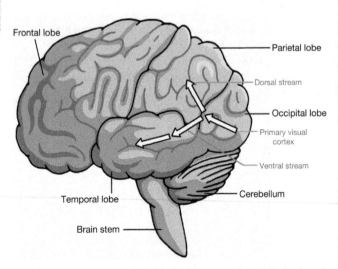

Frontal lobe

Parietal lobe

Dorsal stream

Occipital lobe

Primary visual cortex

Ventral stream

Cerebellum

Temporal lobe

Brain stem

7. The ventral stream is mainly involved in perception while the dorsal stream coordinates fast visuo-motor control.

visuo-motor control. This means that fast, visually guided actions, such as returning a serve, catching a ball, or jumping out of its way can happen long before you can recognize it as a ball. DF's case now makes sense. It is best described not as a dissociation between vision and consciousness, but between action and perception. She has lost much of the ventral stream that leads to visual perception but retains the dorsal stream needed for accurate visuo-motor control. Many other experiments confirm this general picture suggesting that our natural way of thinking about vision must be wrong.

In the 1970s, Oxford neuropsychologist Lawrence Weiskrantz made an even more extraordinary discovery. He was working with a patient called DB, who had damage to his V1. In this area, cells are laid out in a map of the visual world, and so damage creates a blind area, or *scotoma*. That is, when the person looks steadily straight ahead, there is an area of the world in which they can see nothing at all. In normal life this may not matter too much because they can always move their eyes around, but in experiments it is easy to demonstrate that if you present them with an object or picture in the blind area, they say they cannot see it.

The odd discovery was this: Weiskrantz presented DB with a display of stripes at various different angles and asked him whether the stripes were vertical or horizontal (Figure 8). Naturally, DB said he had no idea because he could not see any stripes. But Weiskrantz made him guess. While still protesting that he couldn't see, DB guessed—and he was right nearly 90 per cent of the time. In other words, he claimed to be blind, yet the data showed that he could see. Weiskrantz called this paradoxical condition 'blindsight'.

Many subsequent experiments have been done with other blindsight patients and with similar results. While denying consciously seeing anything, some can move their eyes towards objects, point to the location of objects, or mimic the movement of lights or objects in the blind field. Others show pupil dilation and other

8. A patient with blindsight can guess accurately at stimuli he claims not to see.

emotional responses to stimuli, and several can correctly guess the colour of stimuli they say they cannot 'see'.

Blindsight looks, at first sight, to be a gift for theories of consciousness. The argument might go like this: the blindseer has objective vision without subjective consciousness; he is a partial zombie who can see without having the qualia of seeing; this proves that consciousness is an added extra and is separate from the physical functions of vision; it proves that qualia exist, and that functionalism and materialism are false.

But things are not so simple. The most likely explanation of blindsight depends on the fact that there are roughly ten separate, parallel pathways along which visual information flows through the brain. Most cells (about 85 per cent) take the major route to V1 but the rest go via minor routes to other cortical and subcortical areas. Since these are not affected by damage to V1 the odd abilities of the blindseer probably depend on using these other pathways. As an example, suppose that a pathway for controlling eye movements remains intact. Then it is not surprising that the patient's eyes move to track an object in the blind field. He may even feel his own eyes moving and so be able to guess that there is an object there. But without V1 he cannot possibly recognize the object or detect its shape, size, or any other features. In this sense he really is blind.

If this is the right interpretation, blindsight remains a fascinating phenomenon, but it does not prove that consciousness can be separated from the processes of vision. If it tells us anything about consciousness, it is that our ordinary concept of a single central visual experience is probably completely wrong. And how any visual experience comes to be conscious remains as far from explanation as ever.

Chapter 3
Time and space

The timing of experience

Could consciousness lag behind the events of the real world? This curious question emerged from research begun in the 1960s by neuroscientist Benjamin Libet. His findings have led to theories about 'Libet's delay' or the 'half second lag' and, as we shall see in Chapter 6, to implications for free will and responsibility.

The earliest of Libet's experiments were performed on patients who had the surface of their brains exposed for surgery and had given permission for Libet to stimulate the brain surface with electrodes. Libet used trains of electrical stimulation varying in length from a few milliseconds (thousandths of a second) to over a second, and what he found was this: with short trains of electrical pulses the patients felt nothing, but with longer bursts they said they could feel something like a touch on their arms. Libet showed that it needed half a second of continuous electrical stimulation for the patient to say, 'I feel it'. It seemed as though the conscious experience came a full half second after the stimulation began.

Confirmation of this odd finding came from experiments using a technique for blocking, or 'masking', conscious sensations. It was already known that stimulating the somatosensory cortex with electrodes just after a real touch can prevent the touch being felt, so Libet varied the timing. If he stimulated the brain more than half a second after the touch then the patient still felt it, but if he stimulated it before the half second had passed then the sensation of touch was obliterated as though it had never been.

The most obvious interpretation (though not necessarily the correct one) was that it takes half a second of neuronal activity to produce consciousness. Libet called this 'neuronal adequacy for consciousness'. This is very odd. It implies that consciousness must lag far behind the events of the real world and so must be useless in responding to fast-changing events.

It is important to realize how long half a second is in brain terms. Signals run along neurons at up to 100 metres per second and cross synapses in about half a millisecond. So the signal from a real touch on the arm reaches the brain in a few hundredths of a second, and sounds get there even faster. The typical reaction time to a flash of light is about a fifth of a second, and that involves many neurons being activated to detect the light and coordinate the response. It seems crazy that consciousness could come so late, but this is what Libet's results seemed to show.

If this is true, why don't we realize it? Libet's own explanation involves the phenomenon of 'backward referral' or 'subjective antedating'. He argues that consciousness does indeed require half a second of continuous activity in the cortex, but that we do not notice the delay because the events are referred back in time once neuronal adequacy has been reached. This is possible because when a stimulus happens—say a flash of light or a quick touch—there is an immediate effect in the brain called the 'evoked potential'. According to Libet's theory, when we consciously feel a touch on the arm, activity builds up in the somatosensory cortex until neuronal adequacy is reached. Once reached, the apparent timing of the touch is referred back to the time of the evoked potential.

Otherwise nothing is felt. In this way no delay in consciousness is ever noticed.

Libet's experiments are unlikely to be repeated because advances in medicine have made that kind of invasive surgery unnecessary. However, they are usually accepted as valid by researchers in the field. What is not agreed is the correct interpretation. Libet himself is among those anti-materialists who believe the results challenge the equivalence of mind and brain. Dualists such as philosopher of science Sir Karl Popper and neurophysiologist Sir John Eccles took the results to prove the power of the non-physical mind; mathematician Sir Roger Penrose and anaesthetist Stuart Hameroff claim that quantum theory is required to explain the results; Libet himself proposed a non-physical, 'conscious mental field'.

Many philosophers disagree. According to both Churchland and Dennett the results only appear to have these peculiar implications because people will not give up their false ideas about consciousness, making the problem seem insoluble when it should not be.

This objection is worth exploring a little more deeply. The natural way to think about the half-second delay is probably something like this. A touch on the arm (or any other stimulus) sends signals along the nerves of the arm to the brain, where they finally 'arrive in consciousness' and the person feels the touch. This means there are two different kinds of phenomenon, each with its own timing. First, there are objective events with actual measurable times, such as when the electrical stimulus occurs or when a given brain cell fires. Second, there are subjective experiences with their own times, such as when the touch is felt or when it 'comes into consciousness'.

This description may seem quite unexceptionable. Indeed, you may be convinced that it has to be true. But note all the trouble it leads us into. If you accept this apparently obvious way of thinking about the brain, then you are stuck either with a place in the brain where physical events correspond to mental ones, or with a time at which unconscious processes mysteriously turn into conscious ones: the time at which they 'become conscious' or 'enter consciousness'. But what on earth could this mean? Thinking this way, you hit right up against the hard problem and the apparently insoluble mystery.

One way forward is to stick with this natural view of consciousness and try to solve the hard problem; explaining how unconscious processes turn into conscious ones. This is the approach that leads to quantum theories, various kinds of dualism, and, indeed, many of the scientific theories of consciousness that we have. Libet's own suggestion is that when neuronal adequacy has been reached brain activity turns into conscious experience, but he does not explain how or why, and the mystery remains.

A much more radical alternative is to throw out the assumption that conscious experiences can be timed at all. Giving up the natural view of consciousness is extremely difficult, but some other odd examples may make the possibility more attractive.

Clocks and rabbits

Imagine that you are sitting reading a book when, just as you turn the page, you notice that the clock is chiming. A moment ago you were not aware of the chimes but now, suddenly, they have entered your awareness. At that moment, you can remember the sounds you were not listening to and count the chimes you did not hear. Perhaps there have been three already and you go on to find that it is six o'clock.

This oddity was noted by William James over a century ago and is particularly powerful because you can check that you counted correctly, but a similar thing happens all the time with background noises. You may suddenly become aware of that drilling noise out in the road. You were not aware of it until that moment but now you can remember what it sounded like before you noticed it. It seems almost as though someone, if not you, had been listening all along. These experiences are so familiar that we tend to ignore them, but they are worth thinking about a little more carefully.

Take the example of the clock. If the ordinary view of consciousness is correct, experiences must either be conscious or unconscious, either in the theatre or stream of consciousness or not. So what about the first three 'dongs' of the clock? If you say that they were conscious all along, then you cannot explain the very definite impression that you only became conscious of them later. On the other hand, if you say that they were unconscious you have to explain what happened when you became conscious of them. Were they unconscious until the fourth dong and then subjectively referred back in time, as Libet might say? Were memories of them held in some unconscious state only to be switched to being conscious when your attention switched? Quite apart from the difficulty of explaining what this switch could mean, this leaves us with a rather odd kind of stream containing a mixture of things that were conscious all along, and others that only got pulled in retrospectively.

Many other examples reveal the same peculiarity. In a noisy room full of people talking, I may suddenly switch my attention because someone behind me has said, 'Guess what Jeremy said yesterday about Sue...she...'. I prick up my ears. At this point I seem to have been aware of the whole sentence as it was spoken. But was I really? The fact is that I would never have noticed it at all if my name had not been mentioned. So was the sentence in or out of the stream?

In fact, this problem applies to all of speech. You need to accumulate lots of later words before the beginning of the sentence makes sense. What was in the stream of consciousness while all this was happening? Was it just meaningless noises or gobbledegook? Did it switch from gobbledegook to words half way through? It doesn't feel like that. It feels as though you listened and heard a meaningful sentence as it went along, but this is impossible. Or take just one word, or listen to a robin singing. Only once the word is finished, or the song complete, can you know what it was that you heard. What was in the stream of consciousness before this point?

An ingenious experiment, called the 'cutaneous rabbit illusion', demonstrates the problem at its most obvious (Figure 9). To get this effect, a person holds out her arm and looks the other way while the experimenter taps up her arm. In the original experiment a tapping machine was used, but the effect can be demonstrated using carefully practised taps with a sharp pencil. The critical point is to tap quickly at precisely equal intervals and with equal

9. The experimenter taps quickly five times at the wrist, three times at the elbow, and twice on the upper arm, but the sensation is like a little animal scurrying up the arm. How does the brain know where to place taps two to four if the tap on the elbow has not yet happened? Is the sensation delayed from entering consciousness? If not, what is happening?

pressure, five times at the wrist, three times near the elbow, and twice near the shoulder.

What does this person feel? Oddly enough, she feels a series of taps running rapidly from wrist to shoulder, not in three distinct bursts as they are in reality, but as though a little rabbit were scampering all the way up her arm—hence the 'cutaneous rabbit'. The effect is odd and makes people laugh, but the questions it poses are serious ones. How does the brain know where to put the second, third, and fourth taps (i.e. running up the forearm) before the elbow taps have even happened? When a stick is laid across someone's left and right index fingertips and rapid taps made on the stick above the fingertips, the intermediate taps can be felt in the space in between, as though on the stick. This is the so-called 'out-of-body rabbit'.

Experiments show that the illusory taps correlate with activity in the somatosensory cortex just where it would be expected if the taps were real, as though the brain is filling in the gaps. This wouldn't account for the stick effect but mathematical models involving predictive processing have been used to explain this and other variants in terms of learned expectations. So in physical terms the illusion makes sense. But where does consciousness come in?

If you stick to the natural idea that any tap (say the fourth one) must either have been conscious or unconscious (in the stream or not), then you get into a big muddle. For example, you might have to say that the third tap was consciously experienced at its correct place (i.e. on the wrist), but then later, after the sixth tap occurred, this memory was wiped out and replaced with the conscious experience of it happening half way between wrist and elbow. If you don't like this idea, you might prefer to say that consciousness was held up for some time—waiting for all the taps to come in before deciding where to place each one. In this case, the fourth tap remained unconscious until after the sixth tap occurred, and was then referred back in time so as to be put in its correct place in the stream of consciousness.

Once again, we seem to be faced with an unpleasant choice: either deal with these problems or abandon the natural idea of the stream of conscious experiences. One last example may reveal yet more trouble in the stream.

Unconscious driving

What is attention? In 1890, William James famously proclaimed that 'Everyone knows what attention is', but many subsequent arguments and thousands of experiments later it seems that no one knows what attention is, and there may not even be a single process to study. Attention is one of those aspects of consciousness that seems obvious and easy to understand at first sight but gets more peculiar the more you study it.

The most natural way to think about attention is as a spotlight that we can shine on some things while leaving others in the dark (Figure 10). Sometimes this spotlight is grabbed by a loud noise or someone calling our name; but at other times we direct the

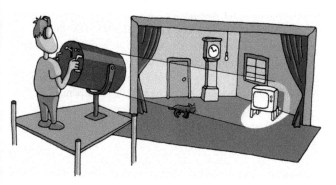

10. Are we like directors, pointing the light of our own attention now here, now there, as we consciously decide?

spotlight ourselves, choosing now to think about the book we are reading and then to look out of the window for a minute or two. This power to direct attention is not only something we value, but it seems to be something that our consciousness does. It *seems* as though I consciously decide what to attend to, but do I really?

If we think about what is going on inside the brain, this natural idea becomes much harder to understand. What could be directing what inside this complex, parallel processing system? Perhaps the best way to think about attention is as a way, or ways, of allocating the brain's resources. So when I concentrate on a conversation, there is more energy and processing capacity given to the auditory and language parts of my brain than to vision and touch; when my attention is on watching a game, more is given to vision, and so on.

Now we may ask, what determines this allocation of resources? Psychologists have done thousands of experiments on how attention is directed, the cues that affect it, and how it varies with age, illness, and even culture. They have studied its relationships with working memory, eye movements, and processing load, and the ways it can be divided or disrupted. They have discovered interesting phenomena such as 'inattentional blindness' (see Chapter 4) or the 'attentional blink' in which people fail to see perfectly visible stimuli if these appear quickly after another stimulus they did attend to. Neuroscience has also provided answers, discovering two attention systems. *Involuntary* attention, when attention is grabbed by events, is dealt with by the ventral attention system located mostly in the right hemisphere in frontal, parietal, and temporal lobes. *Voluntary* and deliberate control of attention depends more on the dorsal attention system found on both sides of the brain in frontal and parietal areas.

So a great deal is known about attention, but what about consciousness? What could correspond in brain terms to the powerful sense that I am in there consciously directing the show? This is just one of many reasons why the relationship between consciousness and attention is so contentious. Despite such great progress, there is no generally agreed theory relating attention to consciousness. Some theorists equate the two, others claim they are separate phenomena. Some claim that there can be no consciousness without attention, or no attention without consciousness, and others disagree.

The unconscious driving phenomenon, something any proficient driver has probably experienced, vividly illustrates the problem. You set off on a familiar journey to work, school, or home, and as you drive you start thinking about something else. In no time, it seems, you have arrived but you remember nothing of the drive at all. It is as though you were completely unconscious of the whole process, even though you were wide awake.

What is going on here? One suggestion is that you were attending to your daydreams instead of your driving. But, if attention is a matter of allocating processing resources, this cannot be true because driving requires a lot of processing resources. On that journey you probably stopped at several red lights and set off again when they turned green; negotiated junctions; kept a safe distance from the car in front; adjusted your speed to compensate for hills, bends, and speed limits; and waved to thank someone who let you pull out. These are all skilled tasks involving vision, hearing, motor control, and decision-making. In ordinary language we say, 'I did it automatically', 'I was not *conscious* of the driving'; but what does this mean? It seems easy and natural to invoke the usual metaphors of the theatre or stream to describe the difference. In the conscious case, all those traffic lights, hills, bends, and other cars were on show in our mental theatre or flowing in the stream of consciousness; in the unconscious case, the daydreams took over the show, and the lights, bends, and cars never made it into the stream.

The problem appears again when we ask what is going on in the brain. Let's consider one small aspect of driving: for example, seeing the light change to red and stopping the car. In both the conscious and unconscious cases, a great deal of processing must have happened in the visual cortex and frontal cortex for planning actions, and in the cerebellum and motor cortex where the movements of hands and feet are coordinated. In both cases, you successfully stopped the car, and yet in one case all this activity was conscious and in the other it was not. What is the difference?

This is what any viable theory of consciousness has to explain. It is time to consider some of the most popular theories and learn how they cope with what I call the 'magic difference'.

Theories of consciousness

I get lots of letters and emails from people who claim to have solved the mystery of consciousness and want to tell me their theory. The vast majority of these theories fall into two categories: either they are dualist, proposing a separate mind or soul, apparently with the view that this is a new and revolutionary idea; or they invoke the wonders of modern physics.

Dualism is always tempting because it fits so well with our intuitions, but very few philosophers or scientists think it could be true. In the 1970s, Popper and Eccles proposed their theory of *dualist interactionism*, which entailed a non-physical, self-conscious mind separate from the unconscious, physical brain and able to influence it through finely balanced interactions at synapses. They explained unconscious driving by saying that the non-physical mind engaged only with the daydreaming parts of the brain, not with the vision and driving parts. However, they could not explain how the interaction works or how subjective experience comes about. As with most dualist theories they invent a separate mind to do the job of being conscious, but without explaining how it interacts with the world—other than by magic.

More subtle versions of dualism are called *dual-aspect* or *property dualism*. These are really forms of monism, claiming that the universe is made of only one kind of substance but that this can be seen from different aspects or perspectives, or has both physical and mental properties. These include Chalmers' claim that consciousness is as intrinsic to the world as matter and energy, but these ideas provide no explanation for unconscious driving.

Theories based in modern physics take a different approach. Some liken such strange effects as non-locality, entanglement, or wave–particle duality to strange effects in consciousness and claim that one can explain the other. Some draw upon the controversial idea that a conscious observer is required to explain the collapse of the wave function in quantum mechanics; but the best known theory is the Penrose-Hameroff model of 'orchestrated objective reduction' (Orch OR). They argue that the tiny microtubules found in every brain cell are not the structural elements described by biologists, but are quantum computers that allow for quantum coherence and non-local interactions in the brain. This, they claim, explains the unity of consciousness and the possibility of free will, as well as Libet's odd timing effects. Yet even if quantum computing does occur in brains (which is highly controversial), this still does not explain subjectivity.

The opposite problem arises in Deepak Chopra's idealist theory of consciousness. Author of *Quantum Healing*, he argues for another popular idea, that consciousness, not matter, comes first. Consciousness, he claims, underlies all matter, creates reality and drives evolution. But, as with all idealist theories, this cannot explain how conscious experience can create a consistent physical world that we all share. Many people conclude that quantum theories of consciousness sound eminently plausible if you know nothing about maths and physics, but that in fact the theories are merely replacing one exciting-sounding mystery with another.

Among more conventional philosophical theories are 'higher order thought' (HOT) theories. These suggest that sensations and thoughts are conscious only if the person also has a HOT to the effect that they are conscious of them. So, for example, the driver's perception of the red light would be conscious only if accompanied by a HOT that they are seeing a red light. HOT theories account for the magic difference without invoking any special consciousness neurons; conscious thoughts are those that have HOTs about them. They also deal easily with some of the odd timing effects because HOTs take time to build up, but there is disagreement about whether any other animals are capable of HOTs, and they cannot account for states of deep meditation in which people claim to be vividly conscious without any thoughts at all.

Neurobiologists Gerald Edelman and Giulio Tononi focused on the informational aspects of consciousness, suggesting that consciousness emerges when large neuronal groups form a 'dynamic core' in the brain, with connections looping back and forth between the thalamus and cortex. This led to the mathematically based theory of integrated information proposed by Tononi and further developed with Christof Koch. The basic principle is that consciousness corresponds to the capacity of any system to integrate information over a vast number of possible states and this capacity is measured by a single variable called Φ (phi). Other theories emphasize the size of neural networks or coalitions, the possibility of some parts of the brain 'observing' others, or the binding of features such as colour or shape into conscious wholes by neurons oscillating in synchrony.

Perhaps most popular have been varieties of 'global workspace theory' (GWT), first proposed by psychologist Bernard Baars in the 1980s (Figure 11). This starts from the idea that the brain is functionally organized around a global workspace (roughly equivalent to 'working memory') with a capacity limited to just a

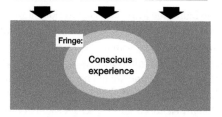

Context operators behind the scenes

| Director | Spotlight Controller | Local Contexts |

Competing for access to consciousness:

the players ...

Outer Senses	Inner Senses	Ideas

Seeing
Hearing
Feeling
Tasting
Smelling
Submodalities
   Heat
   Vibration
	Visual Imagery
	Inner Speech
	Dreams
	Imagined Feelings
		Imaginable Ideas
		Verbalized Ideas
		Fringe Conscious
		Intuitions

the spotlight of attention shining on the stage of working memory ...

Fringe:

Conscious experience

Time and space

Working memory receives conscious input, controls inner speech, uses imagery for spatial tasks, all under voluntary control.

the unconscious audience ...

Memory systems:

Lexicon
Semantic networks
Autobiographical
& declarative memory
Beliefs, knowledge
of the world, of
oneself and others.

Interpreting conscious contents:

Recognizing objects, faces, speech, events. Syntactic analysis. Spatial relationships. Social inferences.

Automatisms:

Skill memory.
Details of language,
action control, reading,
thinking, and
thousands more ...

Motivational systems:

Is the conscious event relevant to my goals? Emotional responses, facial expressions, preparing the body for action. Managing goal conflicts.

11. According to Baars, the contents of consciousness are the contents of a global workspace corresponding to the brightly lit stage in the theatre of the mind.

few items. GWT depends heavily on the theatre metaphor. The very few items that are in consciousness at any one time correspond to those in the bright spot at the centre of the stage, lit up by the spotlight of attention, and surrounded by a less conscious fringe. Beyond the stage is an unconscious audience sitting in the dark with numerous unconscious contextual systems that shape the events happening on the stage.

According to GWT, items are conscious only when being processed within the workspace and broadcast to the rest of the (unconscious) system. So when you are driving consciously, the information about red lights and other cars is in the global workspace and broadcast to the rest of the brain making it available to influence behaviour, speech, and memory. When your workspace is filled with daydreams, the lights and cars are relegated to the fringe, or even to the darkness, and are not broadcast. Theories building on GWT include the neuronal global workspace model developed by French neuroscientist Stanislas Dehaene and implemented in computer models.

GWTs have been popular and influential, but there are two dramatically different ways of interpreting them. In one version, items 'become conscious' by virtue of being broadcast. In other words something changes and a previously unconscious item becomes a subjective experience. The alternative is that nothing changes and the broadcast is all there is. This is what Dennett means by 'cerebral celebrity' or 'fame in the brain'. There is nothing more to being famous than being widely known; likewise there is nothing more to being conscious than being widely available to further thought or action. It is often hard to know which interpretation people mean when they write about GWT, but it's important to note that, in the first version, the hard problem remains: something magical happens to turn unconscious items into conscious ones. In the second, it disappears, but we have to give up the idea that some items are conscious and others not.

This interpretation is one way of escaping the hard problem—not by becoming a mysterian and saying that we feeble humans can never understand such a great mystery, but instead by claiming that both the theatre and consciousness are illusions. This is not to say that consciousness does not exist but that it is not a mysterious extra something with functions and effects that need explaining.

In his 'multiple drafts theory', Dennett throws out altogether the idea that the mind is like a theatre, or even that some things are in our consciousness while others are not. According to Dennett the brain processes multiple, parallel descriptions of the world all the time, and none of them is either 'in' or 'out' of consciousness. When the system is probed in a certain way—say by asking someone to answer a question or respond to a stimulus—he may decide what he is conscious of and tell you about it. But up to that point there was no truth of the matter about whether that thing was, or was not, 'in consciousness'.

This theory is deeply counter-intuitive; it rejects our conviction that we all know exactly what we are conscious of—or which qualia we are experiencing—at any time. But it has the advantage of coping very well with the peculiar timing effects we have met here. Libet's delay occurs because it takes time for information to become available to a verbal probe; the chimes of the clock were never either in or out of consciousness; driving unconsciously is really 'rolling consciousness with swift memory loss'. So the problems do not arise. But doesn't this do away with the very phenomenon we are trying to explain? Some people think so and accuse Dennett of 'explaining away' consciousness (Box 3).

I disagree. There is obviously something we call 'consciousness' that demands explanation. But is it really the unified stream of experiences we think it is? I suspect that we may have to give up the idea that each of us knows what is in our consciousness now, and accept that we might be deeply deluded about our own minds.

Box 3 What are you conscious of now?

You may be sure that you know exactly what is in your consciousness now, but do you? For many years I have encouraged my students to ask themselves a series of increasingly difficult questions hundreds of times a day, such as 'Am I conscious now?', 'Who is conscious now?', or 'Did I do that consciously?'. Typically, they go from being sure they know the answers to having serious doubts. They realize that asking the question makes a difference.

'What was I conscious of a moment ago?' is particularly interesting, and I have devoted many hours' meditation to it. If there really is a stream of consciousness and a difference between conscious and unconscious processes, then there should be one answer—I was conscious of this, not that. But once you start seriously looking, you find that you can look back and pick up any of several different threads—such as the noise of the traffic, the feeling of breathing, or the colour of the grass. At first, picking one seems to chase away the others, but, with practice, consciousness changes. It becomes clear that there are always lots of threads going on at once, and none is really 'in' consciousness until it is grasped.

Could exploring consciousness like this change consciousness itself? If so, could we be deluded about our own minds, and could we see through the delusion?

Chapter 4
A grand illusion

The nature of illusion

Is consciousness an illusion? The possibility that we might be seriously wrong about our own minds pops up in many guises—that free will is an illusion; that the Cartesian theatre is an illusion; that self is an illusion; and that vision is a 'grand illusion'.

We should first be clear about this word 'illusion'. The dictionary defines it as:

> The fact or condition of being deceived or deluded by appearances . . .
> a false conception or idea; a deception, delusion, fancy.
>
> (*Oxford English Dictionary*)

Or:

> Perception of something objectively existing in such a way as to
> cause misinterpretation of its actual nature.
>
> (*Webster*)

In other words, an illusion is not something that does not exist but something that is not the way it seems.

Most familiar are visual illusions like that in Figure 12. This tunnel creates the impression of a big, fierce man chasing a small,

12. An illusion is something that is not what it seems. In this visual illusion the upper man looks larger than the lower one and may even look more threatening. Yet they are identical.

terrified one, when in fact the two are identical. This simple illusion works because automatic mechanisms in the visual system treat the tunnel as receding in depth. This means that one man appears to be further away than the other and so must be larger. In this, and many other visual illusions, we can see how the trick works and remind ourselves not to be fooled again, yet the visual impression keeps coming back.

Could something similar apply to the whole of consciousness? The claim is not that consciousness does not exist, but that it is not what it seems; that our intuitions are misleading us. If so, perhaps we should throw them out. This is hard to do but, given the trouble we get into when trying to understand consciousness, the effort might be worthwhile.

To pursue this idea, we must start from the way consciousness seems and then consider why this might be wrong. One powerful temptation is to imagine the mind as a theatre (we have already considered why this might be false). Another is to think that consciousness is some kind of force or power, and that we need it for the cleverest or most difficult things we do. Good examples might be creative thinking, decision-making, and problem-solving, but in fact it turns out that some of these can best be done unconsciously.

Here is a simple example: a children's riddle.

> One sunny day I was walking across a field when I came upon an old scarf, a carrot, and two pieces of coal lying in the grass. How did they get there?

If you cannot solve this one straight away, you should try struggling with it; think all around it, try to work out the answer consciously, conjure up a really vivid image of the scene and do your best. The answer really is obvious once you get it. If you still cannot see it, then just let the problem 'incubate' and see what happens. (The answer is at the end of the chapter; but don't look now.)

Studies of incubation show that when people first work on a problem and then drop it to think about something else, the answer sometimes just pops up with no conscious effort at all. Something similar happens with creative artists and scientists. Brilliant innovations and solutions to scientific problems do not appear by magic; what usually happens is that the scientist or inventor struggles for hours, days, or even years with a difficult problem, putting all the pieces together, working out the difficulties, but failing to find a solution. Then they stop struggling, think about something else, and all of a sudden, 'pop', the solution appears—a eureka moment! It is as though some part of the mind has been working away and found the solution on its own.

Experiments have also explored special problems that are too complex to solve by logical thinking, yet can be solved. They require something else; something we might call intuition. In a famous study, people played a computer game that simulated sugar production in a factory. They could control variables such as the number of workers and their pay, but had no idea of the equations that ran the simulation. Very quickly they got better at stabilizing sugar production, but they had no idea how they did it. In fact, those who thought they knew what they were doing performed worse at the task than those who did not.

Something similar is probably going on all the time in our highly complex social worlds. We meet someone new, see their face, clothes, and gestures, hear their voice, and quickly judge them as friendly or cold, trustworthy or dubious, intelligent or not, but how? Along with all our innate abilities we have a lifetime's history of meeting people and seeing how they turned out. We could not possibly remember all this explicitly, or work out the equations for the probabilities involved, but somewhere in the system all this is being done and we end up making surprisingly reliable judgements.

This kind of implicit processing explains much of what we call emotional decision-making, or intuition, for we do not know where the answers come from—we just seem to feel what is right, or 'know' what to do. These important skills have historically been overlooked with rationality admired at the expense of the emotions: the mind elevated over the body. Neuroscientist Antonio Damasio called this 'Descartes' Error', giving evidence that the ability to feel emotions is intrinsic to thinking and decision-making. For example, people with frontal lobe damage sometimes become emotionally flat, but, rather than becoming super-rational decision-makers, they become indecisive and unable to make up their minds.

This shift has now gone much further. Traditional cognitive science, based on brain–computer analogies, has given way to 'embodied cognition', 'situated cognition', 'enactivism', and the idea of the 'extended mind', in which thinking and consciousness depend on a brain that is thoroughly embedded in, and constantly interacting with, its body and environment.

This shift makes sense of how much we are influenced by things we are not aware of: that is, by subliminal (or under-the-threshold) stimuli. Subliminal perception has had a bad reputation, perhaps because of claims that advertisers could manipulate us by inserting very brief messages into films or television programmes. In fact, people's buying behaviour is hardly affected. Nor do subliminal audio messages work in the dramatic ways sometimes claimed for them. Yet subliminal perception is a real phenomenon. For example, when people are primed with a word flashed too briefly to see it consciously, the word can still affect their reactions. So if 'river' is briefly flashed, the next word 'bank' is more likely to be interpreted as a river bank than a place to keep money. Similarly, if smiling or frowning faces are briefly flashed before a meaningless squiggle, people are more likely to respond positively to the squiggle after a smiley face. These and many other experiments imply that all the time we are affected by countless unnoticed events going on around us. Our clever brains process all this information in fantastically complex ways, and yet we consciously know little about it.

The temptation is to imagine something like this: the human mind consists of a vast unconscious part, some smaller preconscious or subconscious parts, and finally the conscious mind, which is what we know about and experience directly. I believe this traditional image has to be wrong.

Filling in the gaps

Have you ever had the experience of suddenly seeing something right in front of your eyes that you had not noticed before—those glasses you thought you'd lost; the dustbin by the door that you walked right past; a snowman in the neighbour's garden? What was in your consciousness before that moment? As William James exclaimed in 1890, 'There would have been *gaps*—but we felt no gaps'. There were no glasses or dustbin-shaped gaps in our world, no snowman-shaped space on the lawn. Had our mind filled in over the gap? Did it need to?

This common experience seems odd, but the reason it seems odd is probably something like this. We imagine that somewhere inside our head or mind there is a complete picture of the world which is our conscious experience. After all, when we look around we see a world with no gaps, so we assume that there must be such a gap-free world represented inside. This idea of an inner, detailed representation in the head was the underlying assumption of most of cognitive science for many decades. Yet it may be wrong to think of our minds this way, as some simple experiments can show.

First, there is the blind spot. The human eye is designed in a most curious way which, incidentally, reveals its evolutionary history. Somewhere in our ancestors' far past, simple eyes developed with nerves from a few light-receptor cells going forwards before going back to the simple brain. Natural selection has to work on whatever is already there, so this primitive eye gradually developed into a variety of complex eyes with muscles, lenses, and thousands of receptors tightly packed together. The neurons would have got in the way of the light, but evolution cannot, as it were, decide it has taken a wrong path and start again. So the original scheme stayed and we have neurons running in front of our receptors before coming together into a big bundle called the optic nerve. This goes out through the retina, making a hole

13. Hold the book out at arm's length. Put a hand over your right eye and look at the small black dot with your left eye. Now move the page back and forth slowly. At some distance you will find that the Cheshire cat disappears. This is because it is now falling on your blind spot.

(about 15° out from the centre) in which there are no receptors. Do we notice this blind spot? Not at all. To demonstrate this to yourself, try the test in Figure 13.

In ordinary life, we simply do not notice these two blind spots. Part of the reason is that we have two eyes, so each compensates for the other, but even when we cover one eye we do not see a hole in our vision. Why not? It is the same question as before. Does the brain fill in the missing bits to cover over the gap? If so, with what? There have been heated debates about this question of filling-in.

Dennett argues that the brain does not need to fill in the gaps with details and does not do so. This is because seeing is not a process of building up a picture-like copy of the world for an inner self to look at; it is more like making guesses or predictions about what is there. This kind of conceptual filling-in happens all the time. Right now you can probably see many objects obscuring others: a book covering part of the desk, the carpet disappearing behind a table leg, scenery obscured by a car. Of course you don't see a car-shaped hole in the scenery—but nor do you need to fill in the missing piece with plausible trees and bushes. Your visual experience is that there *is* continuous scenery even though you cannot see it all.

Dennett now asks us to imagine walking into a room papered all over with identical portraits of Marilyn Monroe. We would, he says, see within a few seconds that there were hundreds of identical portraits, and would quickly notice if one had a hat or a silly moustache. Our natural conclusion is that we must now have a detailed picture of all those Marilyns in our head. But, says Dennett, this cannot be so. Only the *fovea*, in the centre of our retina, sees clearly, and our eyes make only about four or five *saccades* (large eye movements) each second, so we cannot have looked clearly at each portrait. Our rich experience depends on texture detectors that can see a repeating pattern across the whole room, and dedicated pop-out mechanisms that draw attention to oddities like a silly moustache or a different colour. So what we see is not a detailed inner picture at all but something more like a guess, or hypothesis, or representation that there are lots of identical portraits. The brain does not need to represent each Marilyn individually in an inner picture, and does not do so. We get the vivid impression that all that detail is inside our heads, when really it remains out there in the world.

Yet filling-in may really happen. Psychologists Richard Gregory and V. S. Ramachandran created artificial scotomas (or blind spots) by asking people to look straight at the centre of a display of flickering 'snow'. Offset by 6° was a small grey square with no snow. At first people saw the square, but after about five seconds it became filled with snow like the rest of the screen. Next, when the whole screen was made grey, they saw a square of snow that lasted for two or three seconds. Other experiments revealed separate mechanisms for colour, texture, and movement. One example had twinkling black dots on a pink background with a square of black spots moving horizontally on grey. In a few seconds the square faded, but it did so in two distinct stages. First the grey changed to pink, and then the moving dots changed to twinkling ones.

Another experiment used a background of English or Latin text. The square was filled in as before but, curiously, the subjects now said that they could see letters in the square but could not read them. This is reminiscent of dreaming in which people may see writing on books, newspapers, or flashing neon signs but cannot read it. So what are they seeing? Perhaps it is more like the *idea* of writing than an area covered with actual letters.

If this is so, we might expect to find corresponding brain activity in higher visual areas which are more conceptual (e.g. V3) but not in the primary visual cortex where the cells are laid out in a way that maps directly onto the retina (V1 and V2). Monkeys respond to artificial scotomas in the same way as we do, and early experiments found that cells in their higher visual cortex did indeed respond as though there were a real stimulus there. Scanning humans with fMRI (functional magnetic resonance imaging) also reveals activity that corresponds to filling-in, but research continues to explore just where and why this happens.

Perhaps touch is a little simpler than vision, and you will remember the cutaneous rabbit that seems to scamper up your forearm between rapid taps at the wrist and elbow. This illusion has been induced with people lying in an fMRI scanner, and the results show that there is brain activity in the somatosensory cortex corresponding to where the illusory 'rabbit hops' were felt. Indeed this activity was similar in strength and location to what would be expected from real taps on the skin.

So we now know that filling-in is a real phenomenon and can be detected in the brain, but just how much is filled in and exactly where it happens remains to be discovered.

Blindness to change

Imagine you take part in an experiment and are asked to look at the top picture of Figure 14. Then, just as you move your eyes, the picture is changed to the one below. Would you notice? Most people are sure that they would. But they are wrong.

This is the phenomenon of change blindness and has been demonstrated in many different ways. The first experiments, in the 1980s, used eye trackers. A laser beam, reflected off the subject's eye, detected eye movements and instantly changed the text or picture they were looking at. People failed to notice even

14. If these two pictures were swapped just as you moved your eyes or blinked, you would not see the change. Experiments on change blindness suggest that seeing does not mean building up a detailed representation of the visual world inside your head.

large and apparently obvious changes. Eye trackers are expensive, so I tried the simpler method of forcing people to move their eyes by moving the picture slightly and changing it at the same time. I found the same extraordinary effect.

Subsequently many other methods have been used. The easiest is to have a brief grey flash between the two pictures; they can then be flicked back and forth, from one to the other, until the observer sees the change. Typically, it can take people many minutes to detect even a large object that changes colour, or one that disappears altogether. This is a most frustrating experience. You look and look and see nothing changing; if you are with other people you hear them laughing; then suddenly you see the obvious and cannot imagine how you could have missed it.

The effect works because all of these methods inactivate the pop-out mechanisms and movement detectors that normally draw our attention to a change. Without those we have to rely on memory across eye movements (*trans-saccadic memory*) and—as these experiments show—memory for what we have just been looking at seems to be surprisingly poor.

But why are we surprised? The reason is probably this. We imagine that as we look around a scene we are taking in more and more of the picture with each glance until we have a rich impression of it all inside our head. This is how seeing feels, and this is how we imagine it must work. But if this is so, we ought surely to remember seeing the railing and notice when the top disappears. The power of change blindness suggests that there must be something wrong with this natural theory of vision; this is why I concluded that 'the richness of our visual world is an illusion'.

Does paying careful attention to something save you from missing the change? Psychologists Daniel Levin and Daniel Simons created short movies in which various distinctive objects disappeared or changed. In one movie, a woman is sitting in a room when the phone rings outside. As she gets up and goes to the door the scene cuts to outside the room and a completely different person picks up the phone. Only a third of observers detected the change.

You might think that this worked by some trickery in the film, but, amazingly, Levin and Simons have demonstrated the same effect with ordinary people in everyday surroundings. In one clever experiment various lone pedestrians were approached on the campus of Cornell University and asked for directions. While the experimenter kept the pedestrian talking, two assistants dressed as workmen rudely barged between them carrying a door. At that moment, the experimenter grabbed the back of the door and swapped places with one of the workmen who had been carrying it. The poor pedestrian was now talking to a completely different person. Yet only half the pedestrians noticed the substitution.

Again, when asked whether they think they would detect such a change most people are convinced they would—but they are wrong. This misjudgement is known as 'change blindness blindness'. Children and those over 65 years old are slower at detecting changes but no one is entirely exempt.

There are implications here for ordinary life. For example, change blindness can be induced by using 'mudsplashes' or meaningless blobs to coincide with the change. This happens frequently on the road and in the air, suggesting that dangerous mistakes might be made by drivers or pilots if a crucial event occurs just as some mud hits the windscreen, and this may well be the cause of some apparently inexplicable accidents. But here we are concerned with the implications for consciousness. Do we walk around constantly deluded about how much we are consciously seeing? (Box 4)

'Grand illusion' theory

The findings of change and inattentional blindness challenge the way most of us think about our own visual experiences: that is,

Box 4 Inattentional blindness

The strange phenomenon of inattentional blindness implies that we may miss seeing things unless we pay attention to them. Psychologists Arien Mack and Irvin Rock asked people to attend steadily to a fixation spot and, when a cross briefly appeared, decide whether one arm was longer than the other. When a highly visible image unexpectedly flashed near the cross, most of them failed to see the image, and when they had to attend to a cross slightly away from where they were looking, they failed to see an image flashed right before their eyes. In other words, they were blind right where they were looking. Mack and Rock conclude that there is no conscious perception without attention.

The most dramatic demonstration is a video called *Gorillas in Our Midst* by Simons and Chabris. Two teams, one in white T-shirts, one in black, are seen throwing basketballs to their team mates and the viewer has to count the number of passes between those wearing white. Meanwhile, a woman dressed in a black gorilla suit walks right through the middle, thumping her chest on the way. Amazingly about half of observers fail to see this large gorilla, probably because they are concentrating on the white players and trying to ignore black. Further experiments with eyetrackers have shown that people can be looking straight at the gorilla and still not see it.

Inattentional blindness can be affected by alcohol, by expectations, and by whether you are doing other difficult tasks at the same time, with important implications for safety. Magicians have played tricks with attention for thousands of years, but experiments like these suggest we may be tricked all the time, consciously seeing only the very few things we are currently paying attention to.

if we believe we have a rich and detailed stream of pictures passing through our consciousness one after the other, we must be wrong. This is the basis of 'grand illusion' theory. This is not to say that *everything* is illusion as in some spiritual traditions, but rather that we are wrong about vision: the kind of visual world we think we have is a grand illusion.

Could we be so wrong? If we are, we need to understand how the illusion is perpetrated and why we fall for it. There are several different theories that try to explain the findings, all starting from the discovery that every time we move our eyes we throw away most of the available information. Obviously we have to keep some, otherwise the world would be incomprehensible, so the theories differ in explaining how much and what sort of information we do retain when we look around the world.

According to Levin and Simons, we have a rich visual experience each time our eyes fixate on something, and from that we extract the meaning or gist of the scene. Then, when we move our eyes, the detail is thrown away and only the gist remains. This means we know roughly what we are looking at and can always look again if we want to see something in detail. This, they argue, gives us a phenomenal experience of continuity without too much confusion.

Canadian psychologist Ronald Rensink has a somewhat different interpretation, arguing that the visual system never builds complete and detailed representations of the world at all, not even during fixations. Instead, it creates representations of single objects, one at a time, as our attention shifts around. Whenever we stop attending to an object it loses its coherence and falls back into a soup of separate features. This way we get the impression of a rich visual world because a new representation can always be made just in time by looking again.

This seems very odd. It is hard to believe that when I am looking at my cat the rest of the room disappears. Yet how could I check?

If I try to look really quickly at something to catch it out not existing, I am bound to fail, for as soon as I attend to it I create a new representation. I can indeed see whole scenes but this is because I can always look again, not because I have a complete picture 'in consciousness'.

This is reminiscent of the trouble William James described more than a century ago when trying to look into his own mind. He likened introspection to 'trying to turn up the gas to see how the darkness looks'. I imagine he would enjoy trying electric lights, or the modern equivalent of trying to open the fridge door really quickly to see whether the light is always on.

With the fridge we can easily check by making a hole in the side or leaving a camera inside, and now neuroscience is making the equivalent possible for our own brains, with important implications for the neural correlates of consciousness. For example, Crick aimed to find the correlates of 'the vivid picture of the world we see in front of our eyes', or what Damasio calls the 'movie-in-the-brain'. But if the visual world is a grand illusion, they will never be able to find them because neither the movie-in-the-brain nor the vivid picture exist in the brain. They are both part of the illusion.

A different way of thinking about the illusion comes through enactive theories of vision. These treat seeing not as a matter of passively receiving information but as an activity. We 'enact our worlds' by purposefully and selectively interacting with our environment.

According to the 'sensorimotor theory of vision' proposed by psychologist Kevin O'Regan and philosopher Alva Noë, vision means mastering sensorimotor contingencies. That is, you exploit the way your own actions affect the information you get back from the world, interacting with the visual input as it changes with eye movements, body movements, blinks, and other actions. In other words, vision is action: so seeing, attending, and acting are all fundamentally alike. What you see is those aspects of the scene that you are currently 'visually manipulating', and if you are not manipulating the world you see nothing. When you stop manipulating some aspect of the world, it drops back into nothingness.

This kind of theory is dramatically different from traditional theories of perception and closer to theories of embodied or enactive cognition. These have implications for artificial intelligence too. Scientists building robots have found that giving robots detailed and complex internal representations is an inefficient and even impossible way of getting them to move around in the real world. Instead, it is better to let them play with the world, make mistakes, and learn for themselves how to interact with it.

Does this help us to understand visual consciousness? Traditional theories, with their detailed inner representations, could not explain how or why those representations become conscious experiences or why we seem to be someone looking at those representations. Sensorimotor theory turns the problem upside down, making the viewer into an actor and the visions into actions. So now it must explain how actions can be subjective experiences. Whether this is an improvement we have yet to see, but it certainly changes the problem. Since the traditional theories lead only to confusion and the hard problem, it is worth taking seriously the idea that vision is a grand illusion.

Answer to riddle:

Children had brought them there to make a snowman that had later melted in the sun. You may have had your own 'eureka moment' when I mentioned a snowman a few pages later; or the answer may just have popped up spontaneously—or not at all.

Chapter 5
The self

Spirits and souls

Who—or what—am I? Answers such as 'I am my body' or 'I am my brain' are unsatisfactory because I don't feel like a body or a brain. I feel like someone who owns them. But who could this be who feels as though she lives inside this head and looks out through the eyes? Who is it who seems to be living this life and having these experiences?

From the scientific point of view there is no need for an owner; no need for an inner experiencer to observe what the brain is doing; no need for an inner self. Brains may be complex and hard to understand, but they are 'causally closed'. That is, we can see how one neuron affects another, how networks of neurons form and dissipate, and how one state leads to another, and there is no need for any further intervention. In other words, my brain doesn't need 'me'.

Even so, I have this overwhelming sense that I exist. When I think about conscious experiences, it seems to me that there is someone having them; that there cannot be experiences without an experiencer. When I think about the actions of this body, it seems that there is someone acting. When I think about the difficult decisions of my life it seems as though someone had to make them. And when I ask what really matters in this world, it seems as though things must matter to someone. This someone is 'me'; my true 'self'.

So we reach an impasse. Science does not need an inner self, but most people are quite sure that they have or are one. And, in addition, many people believe that doing away with the idea of the self would unleash chaos, undermine motivation, and destroy the moral order. Much hangs on whether we believe in the existence of selves or not, yet our ideas about self tend to be deeply confused.

Philosopher Derek Parfit tries to sort out some of the confusion by distinguishing between ego theories and bundle theories. He starts from the undoubted fact that we *seem* to be single, continuous selves who have experiences, and asks why. Ego theorists reply that this is because it is literally true: we really are continuing selves. Bundle theorists, by contrast, reply that it is not true, and the experience of self must be explained some other way.

Bundle theories take their name from the work of the philosopher David Hume (1711–76), who described how he stared into his own experiences looking for the experiencing self but all he ever found was the experiences. He concluded that the self is not an entity but more like a 'bundle of sensations'; one's life is a series of impressions that seem to belong to one person but are really just tied together by memory and other relationships.

Note that Cartesian dualism is only one form of ego theory, and you need not be a dualist to believe in a continuous self. Indeed, as we shall see, many modern scientific theories that reject dualism still attempt to explain the self in terms of enduring structures in the brain. To the extent that these seek a unified and continuing self, they are also ego theories.

The major religions provide clear examples of each type. Almost all are straightforward ego theories: based on the assumption that selves exist, whether those selves are conceived of as souls, spirits, the Atman, or anything else. The existence of such personal selves underlies doctrines about identity, life after death, and moral responsibility, and is central to the beliefs of Christians, Jews, Muslims, and Hindus. Although there are some scientists who are religious, and some who claim that there is no incompatibility between science and religion, the question of self is an obvious sticking point. If each person has a spirit or soul, as well as a brain, then science ought to be able to detect it, but so far it has not. This is not to say that it never will, but certainly there is a problem.

Among major religions, Buddhism alone rejects the idea of a persisting self. The historical Buddha lived in northern India about 2,500 years ago and supposedly became enlightened after long meditation under a tree. He rejected the prevailing religious doctrines of his time, including the eternal inner self or Atman. Instead, he taught that human suffering is caused by ignorance and in particular by clinging to a false notion of self; the way out of suffering is to drop the desires and attachments that keep recreating the self. Central to his teaching, therefore, is the idea of *anatta* (no-self). This is not to say that the self does not exist, but that it is illusory—not what it seems. Rather than being a persisting entity that lives a person's life, the self is just a conventional name given to a set of elements. He also taught that everything is dependent upon prior causes and nothing arises independently; as in the modern idea that the universe is interdependent and causally closed. This explains how he could claim that 'Actions exist, and also their consequences, but the person that acts does not'. Parfit refers to the Buddha as the first bundle theorist.

Bundle theory is hard to accept. It means completely throwing out any idea that you are an entity who has consciousness and free will, or who lives the life of this particular body. Instead, you have to accept that the word 'self', useful as it is, refers to nothing that is real or persisting; it is just an idea or a word. And as for the self who has experiences, this sort of self is just a fleeting impression that arises along with each experience and fades away again. The illusion of continuity occurs because each temporary self comes along with memories that give an impression of continuity.

Such a counter-intuitive theory would probably not be worth considering were it not for the enormous difficulty we must otherwise face in deciding just what a self is. The idea of self as an illusion is at least worth bearing in mind while we look at some of the stranger phenomena of selfhood.

Splitting brains

What would it be like to have your brain cut in half? This may sound like a thought experiment, but in fact, in the 1950s and 1960s, this drastic operation was performed on people with epilepsy whose life was made unbearable by almost continuous seizures. Today they can be treated with drugs or less invasive surgery, but then the only option was to separate the two halves of the brain, so preventing the seizures spreading from one side to the other. In most of these patients the main connection between the two hemispheres, the *corpus callosum*, was severed, leaving the brain stem and some other connections intact. So it is an exaggeration to say that their brains were cut in half, but without the corpus callosum most of the usual traffic between right and left hemisphere stops.

What happened? Remarkably, very little happened; the patients recovered well and seemed to live a normal life, with little or no change in personality, IQ, or verbal ability. But in the early 1960s, psychologists Roger Sperry and Michael Gazzaniga performed experiments that revealed some extraordinary effects.

The experimental design depends on knowing how the sense organs are connected to the brain. Information from the right ear goes to the right hemisphere (and left to left), but in vision information from the left side of the visual field goes to the right hemisphere (and vice versa), as in Figure 15. This means that if you look straight ahead, everything seen to the left goes to the right hemisphere and everything on the right goes to the left hemisphere. Things are also crossed over for the body, with the left half of the body controlled by the right hemisphere (and vice

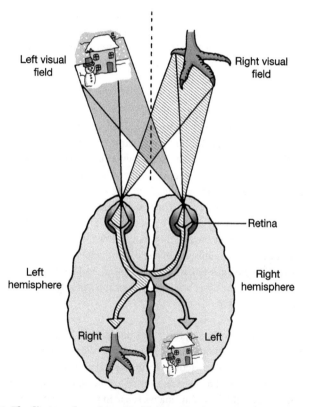

15. The diagram shows how visual information is sent from one visual field to the opposite side of the brain, crossing over in the optic chiasm. Split brain patient PS was shown a snow scene to the left and a chicken claw to the right, but the speaking left hemisphere could see only the chicken claw.

versa). Normally the two hemispheres are connected, so that information quickly gets through to both halves, but in a split-brain patient they are not. Knowing this, the experimenters could communicate separately with each of the two hemispheres of the one person. Would the two halves behave like two separate people? Was each independently conscious?

In a typical experiment the patient sat in front of a divided screen and looked steadily at the centre. Words or pictures were then flashed to one side or the other, thus sending information to only one hemisphere. The patient could respond verbally, or by using either hand.

Suppose that a picture was flashed to the right visual field. Since speech in most people is restricted to the left hemisphere, the patient could then describe it, quite normally, but if it was flashed on the left side, he could not. This showed that the left hemisphere, with its ability to speak, could see only what was shown on the right. Meanwhile, the right hemisphere could see only what was on the left. This was revealed by asking patients to respond without words. For example, they were given a bag full of various objects and asked to select the one they had seen using their left hand. In this way, the two hemispheres could simultaneously give different answers to the question 'what can you see?' And neither seemed to know what the other was doing. Does this make them two conscious people?

In a famous experiment, the split-brain patient PS was shown a snow scene to the left and a chicken claw to the right and asked to pick out matching pictures from an array in front of him. With his left hand he chose a shovel (for the snow) and with his right hand a chicken. This makes sense in terms of what each half saw, but when asked to explain his reasons, he (i.e. the speaking left brain) said, 'Oh, that's simple. The chicken claw goes with the chicken, and you need a shovel to clean out the chicken shed.'

In this way, the verbal left brain covered up its ignorance by confabulating. It did the same when the right half was shown an emotionally evocative picture—making up a plausible excuse for laughing, smiling, blushing, or whatever emotional reaction had been provoked. This might help to explain how these patients can appear so normal. But it should also make us wonder about ourselves. Our brains consist of lots of partly independent modules, and the verbal part does not have access to everything that goes on, yet it frequently supplies convincing reasons for our actions. How many of these are plausible confabulations rather than true reasons, and can we tell?

From these experiments, Sperry concluded that his patients had two conscious entities in one head; each having private sensations and free will. In contrast, Gazzaniga argued that only the left hemisphere sustains 'the interpreter', which uses language, organizes beliefs, and ascribes actions and intentions to people. Only this hemisphere has 'high-level consciousness'.

Which is correct? The trouble is that we have no idea how to find out. We can ask each hemisphere, but—as with other people, babies, or animals—we still cannot know whether they are having conscious experiences as well as speaking and choosing pictures. This brings us right back to the arguments in Chapter 1. If you think that consciousness is an added extra, then you naturally want to know whether both halves have it or whether one is a zombie—but you cannot find out. Similarly, when it comes to selfhood—if you believe in the existence of persisting selves then you naturally want to know whether both halves have a self—but you cannot find out (Box 5).

This seems to matter. It seems to matter whether there is a second conscious self trapped inside the split-brain and unable to communicate—it sounds terrible. But according to Parfit this whole problem is a fantasy provoked by believing in egos. Bundle theory does away with the problem altogether. There is neither one self nor two selves inside the split brain; there are experiences but there is no one who is having them—just as it is with you or me.

Box 5 Would you press the button?

Do you believe in the existence of selves? Does your heart tell you one thing and your intellect another? This philosophers' thought experiment is a good way to find out.

Imagine a machine that you can step inside and travel anywhere you wish to go (Figure 16). When you press the button, every cell of your body is scanned, destroyed, and recreated at your chosen destination. Since this is a thought experiment we must assume that the procedure is 100 per cent safe and reversible. So you can have no legitimate fears about getting lost on the way. The question is—would you go?

16. The teletransporter is a classic philosophers' thought experiment.

If you are really a bundle theorist you should have no qualms at all. Every cell of your body will be just the same after the journey and all your memories will be intact. You will appear unchanged

Hypnosis and dissociation

Imagine the scene. You are at a show, and a hypnotist calls for
volunteers to join him on the stage. Not daring to go yourself,
you watch as lots of people raise their hands and the hypnotist
slowly weeds them out with games and tests until he has half a
dozen or so ready for a 'deep trance'. Some minutes later, after
suggestions of sleep, visualizing beautiful scenes, or imagining
going down in a lift, the volunteers are all slumped and ready
for the fun. In no time, one of them is looking through imaginary
clothes-removing glasses, another is behaving like a circus horse,
and a third is roaming through the audience asking them to
wake him up.

Or consider hypnosis as therapy. It is used to help people give
up smoking, lose weight, reduce stress, or deal with emotional
difficulties, and although many of the claims are exaggerated,
some of these treatments do help. Hypnosis is also used to
reduce pain, and as an alternative to anaesthetic, in some kinds
of operation.

Hypnosis emerged from the discredited *mesmerism*, with its
theory of 'animal magnetism', and had its heyday in the late
19th century, when it was used in medicine and psychiatry, and
for entertainment. Spiritualism was also popular, and psychical

researchers sometimes hypnotized mediums in order to
dissociate their spirit from their body.

Another phenomenon suggesting dissociation was the strange
case of multiple personality. In 1898, Miss Christine Beauchamp,
suffering from pain, anxiety, and fatigue, consulted Dr Morton
Prince of Boston. Prince hypnotized the young woman, producing
a very passive personality. Then a completely new personality
appeared, and began referring to Christine as 'she'. Sally, as she
came to be called, was lively, fun, outspoken, strong, and healthy;
Christine was dull, nervous, weak, and exceedingly virtuous. When
Christine wrote sensible letters, Sally would emerge only to tear
them up. When Christine refused to smoke, Sally would take over
and light up. In other words, Sally made life hell for Christine,
and yet they both inhabited the same body.

The case of Miss Beauchamp was one of the classics of multiple
personality, and hundreds of cases were reported between 1840
and 1910. Psychiatrists, doctors, and researchers all believed that
two or more distinct personalities could take over one body. William
James, for example, thought that such cases proved that one brain
could sustain many conscious selves, either alternately or at the
same time. These were called co-*consciousnesses* or *underselves*.

The cases became more bizarre, with increasing numbers of
personalities and no theory to explain them, provoking a backlash
with experts claiming that the whole phenomenon had been
created by hypnosis and by the persuasive power of male doctors
over their obliging female patients. It was true that many were
induced by hypnosis but some occurred spontaneously and
continued to fascinate people, as with the 1950s film *The Three
Faces of Eve* and the popular 1970s story of Sybil, 'a woman
possessed by sixteen separate personalities'.

These cases heralded a new epidemic, and by 1990 more than
20,000 cases had been diagnosed in the USA, with TV and books

contributing to their spread. Once again, professionals became critical and the cases reduced although some continued, often in people who were seriously abused as children. In 1994, the term 'multiple personality' was replaced by 'dissociative identity disorder'.

Do these strange cases prove that minds can be split or dissociated into parts? The traditional Victorian view treated hypnosis as a dissociated state in which the hypnotist takes control and speaks directly to the dissociated part of the mind, causing the somnambulist (as they were often called) to behave and think differently, and even to perform feats that would be impossible in their normal waking state.

Critics objected that hypnotic trances were faked, or that hypnotic subjects were just complying with the experimenter or playing a role. This same argument carried on through most of the 20th century, circling around one main question: Is hypnosis a special state of consciousness—perhaps a dissociated state—or not? 'State theorists' say yes; 'non-state theorists' say no.

To test the two theories, experiments have compared hypnotized subjects with control subjects who are asked to fake being hypnotized, or to imagine the hypnotic suggestions without any induction procedure. The argument is that if controls show the same phenomena as 'really hypnotized' subjects, the idea of a special hypnotic state is redundant. Many experiments have shown no differences between the groups, which tends to support non-state theory.

Supporting the state view is a strange effect found in the 1970s by psychologist Ernest Hilgard. Experiments had shown that good hypnotic subjects deny feeling pain when their hand is immersed in freezing water (a harmless method of inducing pain, commonly used in psychology experiments). Hilgard believed that, deep down, some part of the person was still feeling the pain and so he said, 'When I place my hand on your shoulder, I shall be able to talk to a hidden part of you...'. When he did so, a 'hidden observer' admitted to feeling pain and anguish, and could describe apparently ignored stimuli or forgotten events. It seemed as though someone else was having conscious experiences all along. These findings led Hilgard to his *neo-dissociation* theory, arguing that in the normal state there are multiple control systems under the direction of an executive ego, but in hypnosis the hypnotist takes over, making actions feel involuntary and hallucinations real. After more than 100 years of research, we still do not know whether hypnosis involves a dissociated state of consciousness or not.

Theories of self

We can now return to asking, 'Who or what am I?', with a little more knowledge but perhaps more doubts because if it is possible to have divided experiences, why do we normally feel ourselves to be unified?

Numerous theories attempt to explain the sense of self, including philosophical theories on the nature of persons, identity, and moral responsibility; psychological theories of the construction of social selves, self-attribution, and pathologies of selfhood; and neuroscientific theories of the brain basis of self. Among these are some with direct implications for consciousness.

William James's 1890 book *The Principles of Psychology* has been called the most famous book in psychology. In two large volumes he tackles every aspect of mental functioning, perception, and memory, and devotes over 100 pages to agonizing over the nature of the experiencing self—'the most puzzling puzzle with which psychology has to deal'.

James first distinguishes between the 'me' who is the empirical self or objective person, and the 'I' who is the subjective, knowing self or pure ego. It is the 'I' that seems to receive the sensations and perceptions occurring in the stream of consciousness, and to be the source of attention, and the origin of effort and will. But what could this 'I' be? James rejects what he calls the soul theory but also rejects the opposite extreme—the idea that the self is a fiction; nothing more than the imaginary being denoted by the pronoun 'I'.

His own solution is a subtle theory, perhaps best understood with his famous saying that 'thought is itself the thinker'. He argues that our own thoughts have a sort of warmth and intimacy about them which he attempts to explain in this way: at any time there may be a special kind of Thought which rejects some of the contents of the stream of consciousness but appropriates others, pulling them together and calling them 'mine'. The next moment another such Thought comes along, taking over the previous ones and binding them to itself, creating a sense of unity. In this way, he says, the Thought seems to be a thinker. This sounds like an extraordinarily modern theory, entailing a constructed self without any persisting entity or ego. However, James rejected extreme bundle theory and still believed in the power of will and a personal spiritual force.

One hundred years on psychologists still battle with the problem of self, Ramachandran calling it 'the greatest scientific and philosophical riddle of all'. Among philosophers, Dennett, having rejected the Cartesian theatre, also rejects its audience of one who watches the show. The self, he claims, is something that needs to be explained, but it does not exist in the way that a physical object (or even a brain process) exists. Like a centre of gravity in physics, it is a useful abstraction. Indeed, he calls it a 'centre of narrative gravity'. Our language spins the story of a self and so we come to believe that there is, in addition to our single body, a single inner self who has consciousness, holds opinions, and makes decisions. However, in reality, there is no inner self but only multiple parallel processes that give rise to a 'benign user illusion'—a useful fiction.

This idea of self as illusion is reminiscent not only of James's theory but of the Buddha's view. Dennett does not make that connection but other thinkers do. Neuroscientist Sam Harris blends science with his own practice of meditation and introspection to conclude that the conventional self is an illusion. Like James, he finds 'no place for a soul inside your head' and rejects any 'unchanging thinkers of thoughts and experiencers of experience'. German philosopher Thomas Metzinger, also a long-term meditator, declares, 'Nobody ever was or had a self'. Yet his 'self-model theory of subjectivity' is rather different. Selves are not things, he says, but 'phenomenal self-models': representations that cannot be recognized as such by the system that created them. Building on the first-person perspective given by our senses, these are models of an inner self looking out at the world. We are deluded because we confuse the model with what it represents.

If these ideas, from the Buddha to the 21st century, are correct, then the self is not what it seems to be but neither is it nothing at all. This illusion of self must have some physical basis and theories differ widely on what that might be. Gazzaniga's 'interpreter' is said to be located in the left hemisphere including language areas, and with different parts of the prefrontal cortex generating and evaluating different explanations. In Baars' global workspace theory the self-system is part of a hierarchy of contexts that determine what gets into the spotlight in the theatre of consciousness and allows information to be reportable and usable. This self-system is also an 'executive interpreter' and located in the left frontal cortex. It is required for what Baars calls 'full consciousness' but what this means remains unclear.

Another example is Damasio's multi-level scheme. Simple organisms have a set of neural patterns that map the state of an organism moment by moment, and which he calls *proto-self*. More complex organisms have core consciousness associated with a core self. This is not dependent upon memory, thought, or language, and provides a sense of self in the here and now. This core self is transient, being endlessly recreated for each object with which the brain interacts. Finally, with the human capacity for thought and autobiographical memory comes extended consciousness and with it the autobiographical self. This is the self who lives your life story, is the owner of the movie-in-the-brain, and emerges within that movie.

All these theories attempt to ground the self in the brain, but they leave the mystery of consciousness largely untouched. In many cases, brain processes are said to be experienced by a self because they are displayed or made available to another brain process, but just how or why this turns them into conscious, subjective experiences remains problematic. Even so, if the brain processes involved can be identified this might help us understand both self and consciousness, and, with the turn of the 21st century, developments in neuroscience began to provide hints.

The default mode network

Have you ever 'lost yourself' in some demanding activity? You might have been writing, painting, sailing, or mountain-climbing when you entered a state of 'flow' in which the self seemed to go into abeyance and all concentration was directed to the task.

This is a familiar enough feeling but its brain basis is only now being uncovered. Far from shutting down when we have nothing to do, the brain is highly active but in different ways from when we are concentrating, and two different brain networks are responsible. Neurologist Marcus Raichle discovered this using fMRI scanning to compare people performing an attention-demanding task with those just resting. Not surprisingly, many brain areas, such as the dorsal attention network, became more active with the task. The surprise was that a network of other areas reliably decreased their activity at the same time. Because the brain seems to default to this state when we rest, this became known as the *default mode network* (DMN).

The DMN includes the precuneus and posterior cingulate deep inside the brain as well as parts of the prefrontal cortex and parietal lobe, all of which have something to do with self, supporting emotional processing, recollections of past events, and future planning. Simple visual experiences are also possible but mainly, when in a relaxed state, we turn to day-dreaming or mind-wandering, and this often revolves around our self with all its worries, hopes, and fears.

Raichle describes the DMN as a self-centred predictive model of the world. This may be essential for running our lives and even for staying alive, but with its focus on self it may also be the cause of pointless rumination, anxiety, depression, and suffering. Meditation and mindfulness have been found to reduce DMN activation beyond levels found with other attention-demanding tasks and to lead to long-term changes in the brain's networks.

So the self, it turns out, is far from being the continuous and unified entity it seems to be. It is not even a continuous and unified model of a self. Rather it seems to be a collection of different models constructed by different parts of the brain. There is the first-person perspective derived from our senses, and positioning us in the world; there is our sense of embodiment or inhabiting our body, and this depends on a 'body schema' maintained in an area called the temporo-parietal junction (TPJ); there is our sense of agency, of being able to control ourselves and influence others; there is ownership, the knowledge that this is my body. Finally, because we have language and autobiographical memory we can bring all this together to tell the story of someone who has lived our life so far and will continue into the future.

If this is so, we have a tough choice. We can ignore the evidence and philosophical difficulties, hang on to the way our precious self feels, and believe in a soul or spirit Alternatively, we can try to live with the knowledge that self is an illusion, accepting that every time 'I' seem to exist, this is just a temporary fiction and is not the same 'I' who seemed to exist a moment before, or last week, or last year. This is tough, but I think it gets easier with practice.

Chapter 6
Conscious will

Do we have free will?

Hold out your hand in front of you and—whenever you feel like it, and of your own free will—flex your wrist.

Did you do it? If not you must have decided against bothering. Either way, you made a decision. You flipped your hand at a certain moment, or you did not. Now the question is, who or what made that decision or initiated the action? Was it your inner self? Was it a thought? Was it the power of consciousness? This may be the way it feels but, as we have seen, there are serious problems with the idea of an inner self, and even if there is one we have no idea how it could make the action happen. So perhaps, instead, there was just a stream of brain processes that determined whether and when you flexed your wrist.

This certainly fits with the anatomical evidence (Figure 17). Much is known about the brain's control of voluntary actions from experiments on both humans and other animals. When any voluntary act is carried out, such as flexing the wrist, the sequence goes something like this: activity begins in the *prefrontal regions* which send connections to the *premotor cortex*. This programmes actions and sends connections to the *primary motor cortex* which sets up precise instructions to move the muscles, with fine tuning

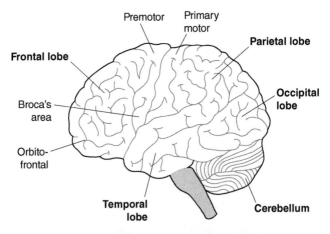

Left side of brain, outside view

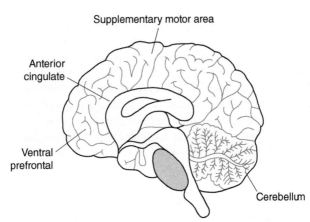

Left side of brain, inside (or sagittal) view

17. **When making a volitional act, neural activity flows from prefrontal areas through the premotor and motor cortex. Other areas marked here may also be involved. Where is the need for consciousness to intervene? How and where could an inner self act?**

managed by the *cerebellum*. In addition, *Broca's area* produces motor output for speech; the *supplementary motor area* sequences pre-planned actions; the *anterior cingulate* and *precuneus* modulate complex actions entailing attention and emotion; inhibitory control is aided by the *pre-supplementary motor area*; and the *dorsolateral prefrontal cortex* is associated with the subjective experience of deciding when and how to act.

So the problem is this. Science can reveal which neurons are active as sensory information comes in, when actions are planned and carried out, and when the feeling of having made a decision occurs. Yet deciding to act doesn't feel like neurons firing, whether in the prefrontal cortex or anywhere else. It feels as though there is something else—my self, my consciousness, 'me'—that makes me free to respond the way I want.

This is the classic problem of free will. In the 18th century, philosopher David Hume called the problem of free will the most contentious of metaphysics. Indeed, it is said to be the most discussed problem in all of philosophy, going back to the ancient Greeks and beyond. The issue raises strong feelings because freedom implies responsibility. We consider ourselves responsible, and we hold others accountable for their actions on the assumption that they freely chose to act the way they did. If there is no free will, then human moral responsibility might seem to be threatened, and with it the rule of law.

Part of the problem lies with determinism. If the universe is deterministic and all events are determined by prior events, then everything that happens must be inevitable, and if everything is inevitable there is no room for free will. Some believe this means that there is no point in my choosing to do anything, and no sense in which I could have done otherwise.

Some philosophers (*incompatibilists*) accept that free will and determinism are incompatible. They argue that either determinism is false (so we can still have free will) or free will must be an illusion (because it would amount to magic—i.e. an impossible, non-physical intervention). Note that adding truly random processes, such as radioactive decay, to an otherwise determined world means the future cannot be predicted. In this case, nothing is predetermined or predestined but there is still no loophole for free will since these processes, if they are truly random, cannot be influenced at all.

By contrast, *compatibilists* find many varied ways in which free will and determinism can both be true. For example, some deterministic processes are chaotic. This means that they can have extraordinarily complex outcomes that cannot be predicted, even in principle, although they are entirely determined by the starting conditions. Also, humans have to make complex choices even in a determined world. Like other animals and some machines, human beings are complex agents and have to make lots of decisions. Indeed, they could not survive otherwise. For some compatibilists this kind of decision-making is quite sufficient as a basis for moral responsibility and the law. And some are happy to count this as freedom of the will.

So where does consciousness fit in? In a way, it is consciousness that gives the whole problem its bite. For some people, it is the human capacity for self-conscious thought that makes us different from other animals and machines; our ability to consciously choose and make decisions that gives us free will and responsibility. Yet this brings us straight back to the same problem. If consciousness is conceived of as a force that makes free will possible, then it amounts to magic—an impossible intervention in an otherwise causally closed world. But if consciousness is not such a force, then our feelings of having conscious control must be an illusion. Some experiments may help us to decide which is right.

The timing of conscious acts

Did you carry out that simple task of holding out your arm and flexing your wrist? If not, you should do so now—or do it again a few times—because this simple action is notorious in the psychology of voluntary action.

In 1985, Libet reported an experiment that is still argued about decades later. He asked the following question: When a person spontaneously and deliberately flexes their wrist, what starts the action off? Is it the conscious decision to act, or is it some unconscious brain process? To find out, he asked people to perform the wrist flexion at least forty times, whenever they liked, while he timed three things: the start of the action, the start of activity in motor cortex, and the time of their conscious decision to act.

The first two of these are easy. The action itself can be detected with electrodes on the wrist (electromyogram, or EMG). The start of brain activity can be measured using electrodes on the scalp (electroencephalogram, or EEG) which detect a gradually increasing signal called the 'readiness potential', or RP. The difficulty comes in timing the moment of deciding to act, which Libet called 'W' for 'will'. The problem is that if you ask people to signal by shouting or pressing a button there will be another lag, and the decision to signal may also interfere with the main decision being measured. So Libet devised a special method for timing W. His participants watched a screen with a dot going round in a circle, like the hands of a clock, and had to note the position of the spot when they decided to act. They could then say, after the action, where the spot had been at that critical moment, and this allowed Libet to determine the time of their decision (Figure 18).

So which came first? W or the start of the readiness potential? You might like to decide which answer you would expect, for this may reveal your beliefs about self, consciousness, and free will.

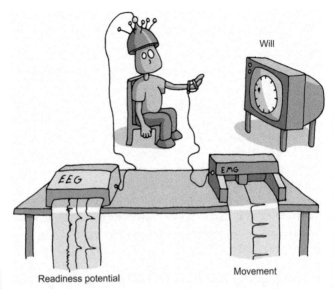

Will

EEG

EMG

Readiness potential

Movement

18. In Libet's experiment subjects flexed their wrist whenever they spontaneously felt like it. He measured (1) RP, the start of the readiness potential; (2) M, the start of the movement; and (3) W, the moment of willing, or the conscious decision to act. The question is, which comes first?

Libet found that the decision to act, W, came about 200 milliseconds (one-fifth of a second) before the action; but the RP began about 350 milliseconds before that, or about 550 milliseconds before the action. In other words, the brain processes planning the movement began over one-third of a second before the person had the conscious desire to move. In brain terms this is a very long time. A lot of neural processing must have happened *before* the person consciously decided to move.

Perhaps it is not surprising that this finding caused so much controversy. After all, it seems to threaten our most basic assumptions about willed action—that our decision to act starts the process off. And yet if you think about it, the idea of a conscious decision beginning before any brain processes would be nothing short of magic. It would mean that consciousness could come out of nowhere and influence physical events in the brain. The only theories that allow for this are dualist theories such as Descartes's, Popper and Eccles's, or indeed Libet's, and we have already seen why dualism appears hopeless.

This suggests that nobody should have been surprised by Libet's findings. Yet they were. Philosophers, neuroscientists, psychologists, and physiologists all entered into long and heated disputes about what these results meant.

Some accepted the results at face value, concluding that consciousness comes too late to start the process of a voluntary action and therefore cannot be the ultimate cause. This, they concluded, shows that we do not have free will. Against this, others tried to reject the validity of the results, for example arguing over the method for measuring W, the task used, or the experimental design, but Libet carried out many control experiments that ruled out most of the problems. And we need no longer rely on these early experiments because later replications have confirmed the findings using fMRI rather than EEG. Some have found even longer delays. In one study people had to choose whether to move their right or left hand and the outcome of their decision could be predicted from brain activity in the prefrontal and parietal cortex up to ten seconds before they were aware of it themselves.

Another objection is that the results cannot be generalized to decisions that matter for free will. Flexing a wrist or choosing which hand to move are hardly comparable with complex actions such as cooking, driving, or choosing a book to read, let alone making difficult choices about whether to accept a job offer or how to bring up your children. In this way, people argued that Libet's results provide no evidence against the kind of free will that matters.

Libet himself did not accept these criticisms; nor did he accept that free will is an illusion. Instead, he found another role for consciousness in voluntary action. He had noticed that sometimes his subjects said they aborted a movement just before it happened. So, in further experiments, he showed that in these cases the RP began as normal, but then flattened out and disappeared about 200 milliseconds before the action was due. From this he argued for the existence of a 'conscious veto'. Consciousness could not initiate the wrist flexion, he said, but it could prevent it. In other words, although we do not have free will, we do have 'free won't'.

This, Libet argued, has important implications for freedom and responsibility, implying that even if we cannot consciously control our desires and impulses, we can consciously overrule them. In this way, Libet was able to accept his own findings without giving up on the power of consciousness. Indeed, he went further and developed the *conscious mental field theory*, which posits that subjective experience is a fundamental property in nature: a field that emerges from brain activity and in turn acts upon and influences that brain activity. This, he claimed, explains the two most difficult features of consciousness—the unity of our mental life and our sense of free will.

Finally, the sharpest criticism is that the experiments are entirely misconceived. As we saw in Chapter 3, experiments on time and consciousness have led to all sorts of muddles and conflicting conclusions. One way out is to take a thoroughly sceptical view about the idea of timing consciousness, not by rejecting Libet's method but by asking whether there even is such a time. The whole idea of timing conscious experiences assumes that there are two sets of timings: the times at which brain events happen, and the times at which those brain events 'become conscious' or 'get into consciousness'. In other words, by accepting that 'W' can be timed, you are accepting that conscious experiences are something other than brain events.

An alternative is to reject this distinction and interpret the experiments differently. For example, if access and phenomenal consciousness are really the same thing, we might say that people reported where the spot was when they knew that a movement was about to happen (i.e. had access to that fact), not when a decision was made by consciousness. In this view, conscious will cannot initiate actions, not because it comes too late, but because it is not separate from the processes going on in the brain and so it is not any kind of power or force at all.

The feeling of willing

All these arguments and experiments cast doubt on the idea that our consciousness is the cause of our actions. Yet there remains the persistent feeling that it is. So it may be helpful to investigate just how this feeling comes about. When actions happen, we have to decide whether we caused them or someone else did, and we can be wrong in two instructive ways. Either we can feel that we carried out an action when someone else did it, or we can think someone else did it when really we did it ourselves.

In 1853, Michael Faraday (1791–1867), the physicist famous for his studies of electricity, carried out a decisive experiment on conscious control. At that time, in the mid-19th century, the craze of spiritualism was spreading right across Europe and America. Mediums put on extravagant demonstrations, claiming to communicate with spirits of the dead through voices, apparitions, and the popular method called table tipping.

For this kind of séance, several sitters gathered round in the dark and placed their hands flat on the table in front of them. The medium then called upon the spirits to make themselves known, and the table would mysteriously begin to move. By asking the spirits to tap once for 'yes' and twice for 'no', or by using more elaborate alphabetical codes, questions were asked and answered, and the sitters went home believing that they had spoken with their lost parents, spouses, or children. In the most dramatic of séances, the table did not just tap with its legs on the floor but was said to tip over, rise up on one leg, or even leave the floor altogether.

Naturally, accusations of fraud were rife, and some mediums were caught with hidden accomplices, telescopic sticks, or invisible strings. Yet some appeared to have no opportunity to cheat, and were restrained by ropes and blindfolds during their performances. Faraday wanted to find out what was going on. After all, if a new force really was involved, the discovery could transform physics. If the consciousness of departed spirits could move a heavy table, then he wanted to know how.

To find out, he glued pieces of card onto the table with a soft cement that would give a little if the sitters' hands moved. He reasoned that if the spirits were moving the table, the card would lag behind the movement, but if the sitters were doing it, the card would move ahead. The results were clear. The card always moved further in the direction the table had moved. In other words, the sitters, not the spirits, were responsible.

Faraday questioned them closely and was convinced that they did not realize what they were doing. In more experiments he used a gauge that showed how much sideways pressure they were putting on the card. When they could see the gauge, all the movements stopped. Faraday concluded that the sitters were not cheating but were using 'unconscious muscular action'; it was the first demonstration that sometimes we can believe we are not doing something when we are.

The same principle applies to the Ouija board, in which a circle of letters is placed on a table, participants put their fingers on the bottom of an upturned glass and then, when asked questions, the glass seems to move without anyone consciously controlling it. This happens because arm muscles tire quickly, making it hard to keep track of where one's finger is. When a slight movement occurs, each person adjusts their finger position, causing a bigger movement. These adjustments are quite normal. Indeed, they are essential for keeping upright when we stand still, or holding a hot cup of tea safely in our hand. No muscles can keep absolutely still, so our body is in a perpetual state of slight movement with constant readjustment.

Note that 'unconscious muscular action' does not imply that something called 'the unconscious' causes the movements. It need only imply that people can perform actions without access to the fact that they are doing so because their body, with all its multiple parallel control systems, just gets on with the job.

A less amusing example occurs in schizophrenia, a serious psychiatric illness involving loss of the sense of personal control. The most common symptom is auditory hallucinations including hearing voices. Some schizophrenics are convinced that spirits of the dead, elves living in the walls, or aliens from outer space are trying to communicate; some believe their own thoughts are being broadcast for everyone to hear; and others that people around them are inserting thoughts into their minds. Brain scans show that the hallucinated voices coincide with activity in the speech regions of the brain, suggesting they are created by the person's own mind. In addition, they show that the brain's response to real sounds is suppressed when the voices are active, perhaps explaining why the voices seem so real. Understanding how this comes about might help with finding effective treatment for schizophrenia.

One final example is a curious experiment from the 1960s, when brain surgery often meant opening up the skull to provide access to large areas of the brain. The British neurosurgeon William Grey Walter had patients with electrodes implanted in their motor cortex as part of their treatment, and he investigated what happened when he asked them to control a slide projector. In some conditions, they could press a button, whenever they liked, to see the next slide. In others, Grey Walter took the output from their brain, amplified it, and used that signal to change the slide. The patients were quite perturbed. They said that just as they were about to press the button, the slide changed all by itself. Even though they were actually in control, they did not have the feeling of willing. Whatever else all this tells us, it certainly shows that *feelings* of willing can sometimes be wrong. So the fact that we feel so strongly that we have free will does not mean that we do—or indeed that we don't.

The illusion of conscious will

Humans are extraordinarily quick to infer that the events they observe are caused by creatures with plans and intentions. Even very young children react differently to objects that move by themselves compared with those that are pushed or pulled by something else, and as they get older they develop what is called a *theory of mind*: the understanding that other people have desires, beliefs, plans, and intentions. It is as though we are set up to detect living things and attribute actions to them. Indeed, this ability has probably evolved for good biological reasons. Survival could easily depend on correctly distinguishing between irrelevant movements and those of a living creature.

Using this ability, we often wrongly imagine that events are caused by an agent, and the success of cartoons and computer games depends on this mistake. Very crude representations of living things can have an audience longing for Jerry to escape from Tom, or poor Kenny not to be killed yet again, and we often speak about inanimate things as though they had minds, saying 'my watch thinks it's Thursday' or 'this laptop is determined to ruin my lecture'. Dennett calls this taking the 'intentional stance'. That is, we treat other people (or computers, clocks, and cartoon characters) as though they had minds, which may be an effective short-cut for understanding what is going on.

Could we be turning the same habit on ourselves when we imagine an inner self who has desires and intentions, and who makes things happen? Could this be why, when we get the feeling of having willed something, we go on to imagine an 'I' who is responsible. As far as evolution is concerned, it does not matter that the centre of will is a fiction, as long as it is a useful fiction.

As ever, we can learn a lot about any process from the occasions when it goes wrong. We have already considered examples in which people caused something but got no corresponding feeling of having done so. On other occasions the opposite occurs.

One example is called the *illusion of control*, and is common in lotteries and games. If people are given a choice over the number of their ticket, they perceive their chances of winning as being higher, and if they do win they feel as though they contributed to the win. Casinos could not make money without the illusion of control, for it is the feeling that their actions make a difference that keeps people playing games of chance. Belief in the paranormal is also bolstered by the illusion of control. For example, if people think hard about something and it happens they may feel that they caused it; if they think all evening of their friend and then she rings, they get a strong sense that their thoughts caused her to call. These feelings can easily override any logical understanding of probability or doubts about psychic powers (Box 6).

Even more powerful is the feeling that our thoughts cause *our own* actions. Psychologist Daniel Wegner likens experiences of conscious will to other judgements of causality, proposing that free will is an illusion caused by a big mistake. This illusion happens in three stages (though they may all occur very fast). First, our brain begins planning an action. Second, this brain activity gives rise to thoughts about that action. Third, the action happens and—hey presto—we jump to the conclusion that our conscious thoughts caused the action (Figure 19).

Box 6 Supernatural beliefs

Why are humans so prone to believing in ghosts, spirits, and gods? Evolutionary psychologist Steven Pinker argues that in seeking to understand the weather, the heavens, or patterns of health and disease, we use brains and perceptual systems that evolved for other purposes. We simply cannot help adopting the intentional stance and so we imagine that someone must have caused the events we see.

The same natural tendency makes spiritualism and psychic demonstrations so beguiling. When psychologist Richard Wiseman re-enacted Victorian séances, his sitters saw objects floating in the dark, felt touches on their skin, heard bells ringing, and were convinced that spirits had been moving among them. The phenomena were faked by a magician, yet even disbelievers fell for the tricks because when we see things moving we suspect someone must be moving them. When objects move just as they would if someone were walking around carrying them, we imagine the person is there. In this way, ghosts and spirits are easily conjured.

So let's suppose that you decide to pick up the phone and ring your friend. First, brain activity begins to plan the action (presumably in turn caused by previous brain activity and external events). This gives rise to thoughts about ringing. Finally, your hand reaches for the phone. You jump to the false conclusion that your conscious thoughts caused the action.

Could it really work this way? Wegner suggests that there are three prerequisites for the experience of willing to occur: the thought must come before the action; the thought must be consistent with the action; and the action must not be accompanied by other causes. To test these proposals, Wegner carried out an experiment inspired by the traditional Ouija board which, like

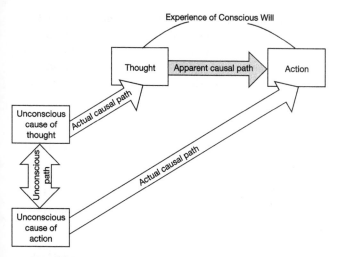

19. Daniel Wegner suggests that unconscious processes give rise to both thoughts about action and the action itself. We then wrongly infer that our thoughts cause our actions.

Faraday's tipping tables, depends on unconscious muscular action. Instead of a glass, two players put their fingers on a little board mounted on a computer mouse which moved a cursor over a screen showing about fifty small objects. They heard words through headphones and had to keep the mouse moving until they heard a signal to stop. In fact one person was a confederate and manipulated the stop, enabling Wegner to show that under certain conditions people were absolutely sure they had stopped the mouse themselves when in fact it was done by someone else. As Wegner had predicted, timing was critical and they were most convinced when they had heard the name of the object just before the stop.

Wegner claims that the illusion of conscious will works just like a magic trick and for the same reason. Just as magicians can force their audience to believe they chose a card or number themselves, we can all be tricked in ordinary life. He concludes that believing our conscious thoughts cause our actions is a delusion. Whether you agree or not, these demonstrations of the mistakes we make show one thing for sure—that the *feeling* of willing something is no evidence either for or against free will.

Living without free will

There is huge resistance to accepting that free will is an illusion, much stemming from the fear that moral responsibility would be undermined and society would collapse. Some compatibilists, including Dennett, argue that without believing in free will we would not be able to hold people to account or maintain law and order.

Yet such fears could be entirely unfounded. People can still take responsibility for their actions. What changes is our attitude to why some people commit crimes while others live kind and selfless lives. When we see that all our behaviour comes from our genes, memes, upbringing, and circumstances, retribution becomes senseless. Rather than punishing people because they are bad, we would ask what good it would do. We might still lock people up to deter them and others from committing crimes or to protect everyone else, and such a basis for law would arguably be fairer and more compassionate. Sam Harris takes this view, arguing that incompatibilism renders hatred irrational while leaving love unscathed. And he takes Dennett to task for caring more about the imagined consequences of unbelief than the truth.

Others worry that if they stopped believing in free will there would be no point in doing anything and they might as well give up. But this does not follow either; nor is it easy to do. If you think you may as well give up then ask yourself just what you will do, for you cannot do nothing. Staying in bed all day is not doing nothing, and you are bound to get up for food or the toilet. Ending your life is not doing nothing, and is neither easy nor enjoyable.

So what are the consequences? Research shows that most people have a traditional belief in free will and this correlates with having more gratitude, higher life satisfaction and meaning, and lower levels of stress. Belief can also be manipulated, and experiments to reduce belief in free will led to lower perceived meaningfulness of life. So clearly there may be a downside to giving up belief in free will. Some people make a compromise, including many of the scientists and philosophers I interviewed for a book on consciousness. They no longer believed in free will but said they had to live 'as if' free will existed, and 'as if' they and others had selves.

Others grasp the nettle and learn to live entirely without free will. In my experience such people become more compassionate and kind rather than less so, and certainly do not sink into torpor or despair. For many of them, initial feelings of despair finally disappear and give way to a greater sense of freedom, the freedom from illusion.

Chapter 7
Altered states of consciousness

Sleep and dreams

Everyone dreams, although some people claim they don't. The proof is easy to come by. If a self-professed non-dreamer is woken when their brain is showing the characteristic signs of REM (rapid eye movement) sleep, they will almost certainly report a dream. So it is dream recall that varies widely, rather than dreaming itself. Another way to demonstrate this is to keep a pencil and paper by the bed and as soon as you wake up write down anything you can remember. The usual effect is a dramatic increase in dream recall.

In a typical night's sleep the brain cycles through four stages of non-REM sleep; going down through stages 1–4, back up to stage 1, and then into a REM period, repeating this pattern four or five times a night. If people are woken during REM sleep they will usually, though not always, say they are dreaming, while in non-REM sleep they may describe thinking, mulling something over, watching rather static images, or nothing at all. Children, and even babies, show the same physiological stages, but the capacity for complex and vivid dreams develops only gradually, as cognitive skills and imagination develop. A great deal is known about the physiology of sleep but this knowledge hides a much less certain picture when it comes to considering sleep as an altered state of consciousness (ASC).

The notion of states of consciousness and ASCs seems superficially obvious. For example, most of us know that we feel different when drunk or delirious with fever, and we may guess that it feels different again to be tripping on LSD or in a mystical state. So we might call all these ASCs. Yet any attempt to define ASCs immediately runs into trouble.

There are two obvious ways to try: objective and subjective methods. Objective measures might include how much alcohol a person has drunk; or which method of hypnosis was used on them. This is not ideal because two people may drink the same amount and one become completely inebriated while the other is hardly affected. Similarly, induction techniques affect different people differently, and some not at all. Few states of consciousness are associated with unique physiological patterns, and measuring brain states gives confusing results. Measures of behaviour might be more useful except that people can claim to have been in profoundly ASCs without their behaviour apparently changing at all. In any case, all these objective measures really seem to miss the point that an ASC is how *you* feel it is: it is private to the person having it.

For this reason, subjective definitions are often preferred. For example, psychologist Charles Tart defines an ASC as 'a qualitative alteration in the overall pattern of mental functioning, such that the experiencer feels his consciousness is radically different from the way it functions ordinarily'. This certainly captures the idea of ASCs but it also creates problems: such as knowing what a 'normal' state is; and dealing with such cases as people appearing to be drunk or delirious while claiming to feel completely normal.

Also, curiously, this definition has a problem with the most obvious state of all—dreaming. In a typical dream we do not feel that our 'consciousness is radically different'—at least not at the time. It is only afterwards that we wake up and say, 'I must have been dreaming'. For this reason, some people even doubt that dreams can be counted as experiences. After all, we do not seem to be *experiencing* them at the time—only *remembering* them afterwards.

This long ago prompted the strange theory that dreams might be instantaneously concocted at the moment of waking up. Two methods have been used to find out. First, it is possible to incorporate features into people's dreams by, for example, playing sounds or dripping water on their skin. Sometimes they will later report having dreamed of church bells or waterfalls. By asking them to estimate the timing of these events, it appears dreams do take about the time they seem to.

Even clearer evidence has come from testing those rare people who can have lucid dreams at will. A lucid dream is when you know, during the dream, that it is a dream. In surveys, about 50 per cent of people claim to have had a lucid dream, and 20 per cent have them fairly frequently. They typically begin when something peculiar happens and the dreamer starts to have doubts—how did I get on top of this building; and why is my grandmother here when I thought she was dead? Instead of accepting the peculiarity, as in most dreams, the dreamer realizes it cannot be real—and with that everything changes. The dream scenery becomes more vivid, the dreamer feels more like their normal waking self, and they may even take control of the dream, flying, having fun, or escaping from monsters. But lucid dreams rarely last long and most people lapse back into the ignorance of ordinary dreaming very quickly.

A few rare, expert lucid dreamers have been studied in the lab and learned to signal from their dreams. In REM sleep most of our muscles are paralysed to prevent us acting out our dreams, but our eyes still move. So these experts learned to signal with eye movements when they first became lucid or to indicate what they were doing in the dream.

This method immediately confirmed that lucid dreams are not brief awakenings but real dreams happening in REM, most often in the early hours of the morning in periods of increased arousal and breathing rate. Scans show that the brain behaves very much as it would if the person were really running down the street, playing tennis, singing a song—or whatever they are dreaming about—and new skills can even be improved by practising in lucid dreams. Scans also reveal greater functional connectivity and long-range connections linking to areas related to self-processing. So this may finally help explain why we feel more alive and more 'ourselves' when lucid (Box 7).

Box 7 A retro-selection theory of dreams

There is no generally accepted theory of dreams, and some very odd facts to be explained. For example, on waking up, we remember having had dreams of which we were not conscious at the time. While experiments suggest that dreams go along in real time, many anecdotes describe dreams that were concocted at the moment of waking up. The most famous is that of the French physician Alfred Maury (1817–92), who dreamed of being dragged through the French Revolution to the guillotine only to wake up with the bedpost falling on his neck.

One theory allows for both these to be true. During REM sleep numerous brain processes go on in parallel, and none is either 'in' or 'out' of consciousness. On waking up, any number of stories can be concocted backwards by selecting one of many possible threads through the multiple scraps of memory that remain. The chosen story is only one of many such stories that might have been selected. There is no actual dream; no story that really happened 'in consciousness'. On this *retro-selection* theory, dreams are not streams of experiences passing through the sleeping mind.

REM paralysis has another consequence—*sleep paralysis*. This happens if you wake up before the REM paralysis has worn off and find you cannot move: a scary experience if you don't know what is happening. Often there are rumbling or grinding noises, eerie lights, sexual arousal, and the powerful sense of someone or something close by. Most cultures have their sleep paralysis myths, such as the incubus and succubus of medieval lore, or the old hag of Newfoundland (Figure 20). Alien abduction experiences may be the modern equivalent—a vivid experience concocted in that unpleasant paralysed state between waking and dreaming.

20. In sleep paralysis all the body muscles are paralysed and only the eyes can move. Most cultures have sleep paralysis myths such as that of the old hag of Newfoundland.

Yet some people enjoy sleep paralysis and even use it as a way of inducing out-of-body experiences (OBEs).

Unusual experiences

From out-of-body and near-death experiences (NDEs) to fugues and visions, a surprisingly large number of people (perhaps 30–40 per cent) report quite dramatic spontaneous ASCs, sometimes known as *exceptional human experiences*.

OBEs are defined as experiences in which the person seems to leave their body and perceive the world from a location outside it. Note that this definition does not necessarily imply that anything has actually left the body—only that the person *feels* it has—and theories differ widely on this point. Some people believe that their spirit or soul has left their body and may go on to survive death. Others are convinced that consciousness can leave the brain. And according to the theory of *astral projection*, an astral body separates from the physical body to travel on the astral planes. Many experiments have tested these ideas but without success. Some have tried to detect the astral body using weighing machines, radiation and heat detectors, animals, and other people, but to no avail. Others asked people having OBEs to look at concealed numbers, letters, objects, or scenes. But although some claimed to see them, their descriptions were generally no more accurate than would be expected by chance. This does not prove that nothing leaves the body, but there is no convincing evidence that it does.

So why do OBEs occur? About 15–20 per cent of the population claim to have had an OBE and most happen on the borders of sleep, during deep relaxation, or in moments of fear, stress, or extreme self-consciousness. Age, sex, religion, and education seem to be irrelevant, but the people most likely to have OBEs score high on *absorption* (the capacity to become deeply immersed in music, films, or other activities) and on *positive schizotypy* (including creativity and a tendency to hallucinations). They are also more likely to dream in bird's-eye view and are good at imagining changed points of view.

OBEs used to be considered beyond the pale of psychology but that changed with an accidental discovery. In 2002, Swiss neurosurgeon Olaf Blanke was operating on a patient with an array of electrodes on the surface of her brain. While trying to find her epileptic focus he stimulated her right temporo-parietal junction (TPJ; Figure 21) and provoked an OBE. Varying the intensity produced either bizarre bodily distortions or full OBEs. What makes this discovery so important is that the TPJ is involved in constructing our body schema, the constantly updated model we have of our body's actions and location in space. When this area is disturbed, whether by electrical stimulation or natural changes in the brain, so is the body schema.

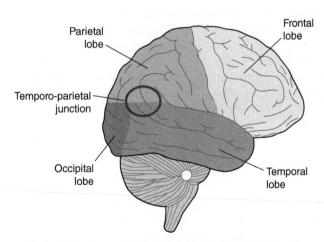

21. The brain has four main lobes: occipital, parietal, frontal, and temporal. The TPJ, as its name suggests, is the area where the temporal and parietal lobes meet. This is where electrical stimulation has been found to induce both bodily distortions and OBEs.

This begins to make sense of OBEs because the TPJ is part of the brain's 'self-system': a network of areas that unites our sense of embodiment with our body image, agency, and personal memories. So OBE research, including simulations using virtual reality, is now helping us understand how the brain builds a model of self.

When people come close to death, they sometimes report a whole series of strange experiences, collectively known as NDEs. Although the order varies slightly, and few people experience them all, common features are: going down a dark tunnel or void towards a bright white or golden light; watching events from above (an OBE); joy, acceptance, and deep contentment; a panoramic review of one's life; glimpsing another world with spirits of the dead or a 'being of light'; and finally reaching a barrier and deciding to return to life rather than stay. Rare NDEs are horrific, with dark voids or hellish scenes. Among people who have a cardiac arrest about 10–12 per cent experience sufficient of the typical features to count as an NDE. NDEs can also occur without any imminent threat of death, as happened to me as a student when I seemed to leave my body for more than two hours while sitting up, perfectly well, and still able to speak. After such experiences people are often changed, claiming to be less selfish or materialistic, and less afraid of death.

Descriptions of NDEs are remarkably similar across widely different cultures and ages, leading to popular claims that this proves the existence of heaven, life after death, or the continuity of consciousness beyond the body. Books about trips to heaven sell millions, yet research shows that the later stages of the NDE depend on an individual's culture, with Christians seeing Jesus or pearly gates, Thai Buddhists meeting yamatoots, and Hindus finding their name written in a great book as they would expect. As for the tunnels, lights, and OBEs, neuroscience is gradually discovering how these can be explained in terms of excessive, random firing in different parts of the brain. This can be caused by stress, lack of oxygen, or even by the brain's own endorphins (morphine-like chemicals) which also induce the positive emotions.

In the visual cortex, hyper-activity produces tunnels, spirals, and lights (as do hallucinogenic drugs that have similar neural effects); in the TPJ, it leads to body image changes and OBEs; in temporal lobes, it releases floods of memories and visions that depend on the person's expectation, prior state of mind, and cultural beliefs. People really can be changed by having an NDE, and usually for the better, but this may be because their brain has been physically changed and because they have contemplated their own death, rather than because their soul has briefly left their body. It seems that NDEs are similar across the world because we all have similar brains, not because we survive death.

Equally profound experiences can happen in the midst of ordinary life. These are usually called 'religious experiences' if they include angels, spiritual beings, or gods, but 'mystical experiences' if they do not. These experiences are usually spontaneous and brief, but can also be induced by certain drugs and with long training in meditation. There is no simple way to define or even describe mystical experiences, which are often said to be ineffable or indescribable. But they typically involve a sense of the numinous, and convey unexpected knowledge or understanding of the universe. Perhaps most central to the experience is a changed sense of self, whether this is a complete loss of the idea of being a separate self or a sense of merging with the universe in oneness.

Drugs and consciousness

The effects of drugs on consciousness provide convincing evidence that awareness depends on a functioning brain. This may seem obvious, but I mention it because many people believe that their mind is independent of their brain and can survive its death. Drugs also help in exploring the breadth of ASCs and how they relate to each other, although we are far from being able to map them in any meaningful way (Figure 22).

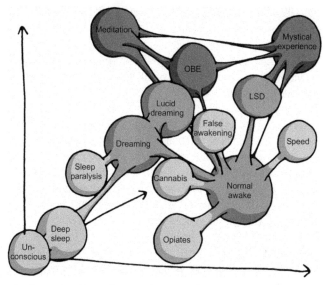

22. Can states of consciousness be mapped? Moving from one state to another can feel like moving in a vast multi-dimensional space, with some states easy to reach and others far away. Many people have tried to develop such maps, but it is hard to know what the relevant dimensions are.

Psychoactive drugs are those that affect mental functioning and are found in every known culture. Some are dangerous and can even be lethal, so most cultures have developed complex systems of rituals, rules, and traditions that limit who can take which drug, under what circumstances, and with what preparation. An exception is modern Western culture, where prohibition means that such protective systems cannot develop, and many of the most powerful psychoactive drugs are bought from criminals on the street and taken by young people without sufficient understanding or protection.

There are several major groups of psychoactive drugs with different effects. Anaesthetics abolish consciousness altogether, the earliest being simple gases, such as ether, chloroform, and nitrous oxide. In low doses nitrous oxide can induce mystical states, philosophical insights, and laughter: hence its other name, 'laughing gas'. Modern medical anaesthetics are more controllable and effective, and usually consist of three separate drugs to reduce pain, induce relaxation, and abolish memory.

Drugs used in psychiatry include antipsychotics, antidepressants, and tranquillizers. Some tranquillizers have become drugs of abuse, as have some depressants, including barbiturates and alcohol (the latter having both stimulant and depressant effects). Narcotics include heroin, morphine, codeine, and methadone. These mimic the action of the brain's own endorphins and are intensely pleasurable for some people, but are also highly addictive.

Stimulants, including nicotine, caffeine, cocaine, and amphetamine, can also be highly addictive, with increasing doses required to have the same effect, and withdrawal causing unpleasant symptoms and craving. Cocaine is normally inhaled into the nose but can also be converted to 'crack' and smoked, which means it is faster acting and more addictive. The amphetamines are a large group including many modern designer drugs such as MDMA, or ecstasy, which has a combination of stimulating, hallucinogenic, and emotional effects.

The most interesting drugs, from the point of view of understanding consciousness, are the hallucinogens. The term 'hallucinogen' may not be entirely appropriate because most of these drugs do not produce hallucinations at all. Indeed, technically, a true hallucination is one that the experiencer confuses with reality—as when a schizophrenic genuinely believes that voices are coming from the walls of her room. On this definition, most hallucinogenic drugs produce 'pseudo-hallucinations', because the user still knows that none of it is real. For this reason, these drugs are also known as *psychedelic* (i.e. mind-manifesting) or *psycholytic* (i.e. loosening the mind).

Cannabis, sometimes classified as a 'minor psychedelic', is derived from the beautiful plant *Cannabis sativa*, or hemp, which has been used for over 5,000 years as both a medicine and a source of tough fibre for ropes and clothes. Many 19th-century artists used cannabis for their work and Victorians used it for medicine, but it was made illegal in many countries in the 20th century. Despite this, cannabis is widely used. It is usually smoked as grass (dried leaves and female flowering heads), as hash (a solid mixture of resin scraped from the plant, together with pollen, and powdered leaves or flowers), or as an oil extract smoked in a vaporizer. Hash or oil can also be used in cooking or dissolved in alcohol or milk. The main active ingredient is *delta-9-tetrahydrocannabinol* (THC), but cannabis contains over sixty other constituents that affect the brain and immune system, the most significant of which is probably *cannabidiol* (CBD), a neuro-protector of which there are high levels in natural cannabis plants but less in modern 'skunk' varieties, making the latter potentially more harmful. Most cannabinoids are fat soluble and remain in the body for days or even weeks.

The effects of cannabis are hard to describe, partly because they are complex and variable, and partly because users say that words cannot convey the changes. Some people become paranoid when smoking cannabis, and harmful effects seem to be increasing as new 'skunk' varieties of the plant are bred for the illegal market. Psychotic illness can even follow, especially among those who use heavily in adolescence. However, for most people the effects are both subtle and enjoyable, including relaxation, enhancement of the senses, increased pleasure in simple sensations, a tendency to laugh, increased sexual pleasure, openness to others, slowing of time, and various effects on memory. Experiments show that motivation is reduced and short-term memory badly impaired, but these effects are usually temporary.

It is perhaps curious that the effects of this most widely used recreational drug sound so nebulous. We certainly have no science of consciousness that can adequately explain what happens to a person's consciousness when they smoke cannabis or why it is so pleasurable to so many.

The major hallucinogens have far more dramatic effects, are usually longer lasting, and are harder to control, which perhaps explains why they are less widely used. They include DMT (dimethyltryptamine, an ingredient of the South American visionary potion, *ayahuasca*); psilocybin (found in 'magic mushrooms'); mescaline (derived from the peyote cactus); and many synthetic drugs including LSD (lysergic acid diethylamide), and various phenethylamines and tryptamines. Most of these drugs resemble one of the four major brain neurotransmitters, acetylcholine, noradrenaline (norepinephrine), dopamine, and serotonin, and interact with their respective function. They can be toxic at very high doses and can exacerbate pre-existing mental illness, but are not generally addictive. Before the prohibition of these drugs, research with psilocybin and LSD showed that they could alleviate long-lasting depression and transform life for the terminally ill. After half a century, research is at last being permitted again and may reveal further uses for these drugs.

The best-known hallucinogen is probably LSD, which became famous in the 1960s when people were urged to 'turn on, tune in, and drop out'. An LSD 'trip' lasts about eight to ten hours; so named because it often feels like a great journey through life. Not only are colours dramatically enhanced, but ordinary objects can take on fantastic forms: wallpaper becoming writhing coloured snakes; or a passing car turning into a dragon with fifty-foot wings. Such visions can be delightful and glorious, or absolutely terrifying—leading to a 'bad trip'. There is often a sense of the numinous, along with mystical visions and a loss of the ordinary sense of self. A person can seem to become an animal or another individual, or to merge with the entire universe. Although there is no known lethal dose of LSD, an LSD trip is not a journey to be undertaken lightly.

In 1954, Aldous Huxley (1894–1963), author of *Brave New World*, took mescaline for the first time and described it as an opening of the 'doors of perception'. Ordinary things appeared colourful and fantastic; everything around him became miraculous and the world appeared perfect in its own 'isness'. His descriptions resemble those of mystical experiences, and indeed some people describe such drugs as 'entheogens', or releasers of the God within.

This raises the interesting question of whether drugs can induce genuine religious experiences. In a famous study, American minister and physician Walter Pahnke gave pills to twenty divinity students during the traditional Good Friday service. Half took a placebo and experienced only mild religious feelings; but half had psilocybin and, of these, eight reported powerful mystical experiences that remained important to them decades later. Critics dismiss these as somehow inferior to 'real' mystical experiences, but this implies that we know what 'real' mystical experiences are.

Meditation

The common image of meditation is sitting cross-legged and going into a state of deep relaxation, cut off from the world. Some meditation is like this, but there are many different kinds, including walking meditations, and alert and active forms.

Meditation used to be practised primarily within the context of religions, most notably in Hinduism and Buddhism, although the contemplative traditions in Christianity, Sufism, and other religions have similar methods. Today there are many secular forms including transcendental meditation (TM) and mindfulness-based stress reduction (MBSR). *Mindfulness* means staying calmly focused on the present moment without distraction, and MBSR is now widely used in schools, workplaces, prisons, and hospitals.

Most meditators sit in special postures, such as the full or half lotus in which both feet (or just one foot) rest(s) on the opposite thigh. Others use easier positions, sitting on firm cushions or a low bench. There is nothing magical about these positions and they all have the same aim: to provide a posture that is both relaxed and alert. In meditation there are always two dangers—either that of becoming drowsy and falling asleep; or of becoming agitated by distracting thoughts or physical discomfort. The special postures help avoid both by providing a firm base, a straight spine, and good breathing.

Now what about the mind? Here techniques differ widely, although it is sometimes said that they all have in common the aim of dropping thoughts and training attention—and neither is easy. If you have never tried it, you might like to do the following exercise—just look down and think of nothing for one minute.

What happens? The instruction cannot be obeyed. Thoughts come pouring up from inside, attention is distracted by events outside, and there is rarely a moment of silence in the mind. Perhaps this is not surprising. After all, our brains evolved to cope with the world and keep us safe, not to go silent on command. Nevertheless, with extensive training it is possible to calm the mind, let go of all distractions, and remain mindfully in the present moment.

Most methods encourage dropping unwanted thoughts. The best advice is not to fight them nor to engage with them in any way, but just to let them go. This can be used as the entire method, but it is not easy and so various other techniques have been developed. Concentrative meditation uses something else to attend to, giving the mind something to do. This might be a *mantra* (a word or phrase repeated silently) as used in TM, or an object such as a stone, flower, candle, or religious icon. The most common method is to watch the breath. The idea is simply to observe one's natural breathing, feeling the air going in and out, and count the breaths up to ten. When you get to ten you go back to one and start again.

Other kinds of meditation use no support. Zen practitioners may sit in front of a blank wall with their eyes half open and practise 'just sitting'—not something many people can do. Meditating with eyes open like this risks getting distracted, although it is easier to stay alert. Meditating with eyes closed risks meandering off into elaborate fantasies or falling asleep.

What is the point of all this? Many people take up meditation to relax and reduce stress but when standard measures of relaxation are taken, such as heart rate, breathing, oxygen consumption, or skin conductance, meditation is found to be no more relaxing than sitting quietly, and reading or listening to music. Indeed, it can be highly arousing, for example when unwanted thoughts keep coming up and you struggle to keep control of your emotions. Certainly, in the short term, it seems that meditation is far from a quick fix, and if you want to reduce stress it is probably better to take more exercise than to meditate.

In the long term, however, the effects are more profound and may be related to changes found in the default mode network and self-systems in the brain. Long-term meditators, who may have practised for many years or even decades, enter deep states of concentration. Breathing rate can drop to three or four breaths a minute; and brain waves slow from the usual *beta* (seen in waking activity) or *alpha* (seen in normal relaxation) to the much slower *delta* and *theta* waves. But people who practise for many years are not usually just seeking relaxation. Their reasons for meditating are usually either religious or mystical. That is, they meditate to seek salvation, to help others, or to obtain insight.

This is certainly so in Buddhist meditation, and in particular in Zen, which has a reputation for using tough methods to reveal direct insight into the nature of the mind. Some Zen students practise silent illumination: calming the mind and looking directly into the nature of consciousness. Others use special stories or questions called *koans*. These cannot be answered intellectually, or even be understood in any ordinary sense, but they can provoke a state of great doubt and perplexity, from which new insights can arise. The ultimate koan is probably 'Who am I?'—a question that turns back on itself and causes the meditator to look deep into immediate experience. Not finding an obvious 'me' is only the first step of what can be a long journey. Along the way, in transitory 'enlightenment experiences', something can break through and the world can be seen in a new way. Ultimately, the illusions of dualism and of a separate self are said to fall completely away.

Such practices raise fascinating questions for the science of consciousness. Is there a standard progression through similar stages or do different people take different routes? Do people really become more compassionate and less selfish after long meditation, as is claimed? And, perhaps of most interest, are any of their insights genuine? In both mystical experiences and long-term meditation, people describe seeing through the illusions of duality and seeing the world as it truly is. Could they be right? Are these the same illusions that the scientific study of consciousness is struggling with? All we can say for the moment is that the study of consciousness is nowhere near sufficiently well developed to answer such questions, but at least we can begin to ask them.

Chapter 8
The evolution of consciousness

It's a lovely day and you are gazing at a great oak tree in the forest. You see the green leaves rippling in the breeze, dappled shade dancing on the forest floor, and birds flying from branch to branch. Looking closer, you see the intricate pattern of bark on the trunk and catch a glimpse of a beetle scurrying to hide. You smell the earth, littered with acorns, and feel the damp air around you. This is your conscious experience. This is how the tree is for you.

But what is it like for the beetle; for those birds; for the hidden sleeping bats above; or the snake hiding in the grass? (Figure 23) We want to know, and it seems reasonable to ask, what the world is like from the animal's point of view. The trouble is we cannot know. As we found when asking, 'What is it like to be bat?', it is no good just imagining you are a bat or a worm. This is the question of animal consciousness. There are really two separate questions here: one concerns which living creatures are conscious and in what way; the other concerns when and how consciousness evolved.

It may help to think about a range of creatures and ask whether they are conscious. Let's begin with a stone lying under the tree. Most people would agree that there is nothing it is like to be the stone, or indeed the lumps of earth lying around, or the pieces of bark that have fallen off the tree. Yet *panpsychists* believe that everything in the universe is conscious; so for them, there

23. What is it like to be an owl; or a spider; or a snake; or a bat? Each of these creatures has senses suited to its way of life and lives in its own kind of world, or *Umwelt*. But are they conscious? How can we know?

are no unconscious creatures, and consciousness was there from the start.

What about the tree itself? Most people would say that trees and other plants are not conscious, yet a case could be made that the first stirrings of consciousness came with having senses and interacting with the world, and trees can sense the world. They respond to gravity, light, temperature, and moisture. Speeding up a film of the tree emerging from its acorn, we would see the tiny seedling twisting and groping upwards, its fresh leaves seeking the light, and we would be much more inclined to grant it the possibility of consciousness. Similar arguments apply to lichens, algae, and bacteria.

What should we place next? If several people try to line up organisms from the least conscious to the most conscious, they will not agree with each other. Some will put human babies near the bottom because they have not yet learned much, while others will put them near the top because of their potential. Some will put chimpanzees high up because they are so similar to us, while others will argue that crows, whales, and dolphins are more intelligent and that intelligence is what counts.

Another consideration is the different senses animals have. Snakes, for example, have an acute sense of smell and some have special sensors that detect infrared to catch their prey. Birds have little or no sense of smell, but they can see ultraviolet light that humans cannot. In fact, many birds have a four-colour visual system, which gives them a much richer ability to see colour than we have with our human three-colour system. What is it like to see a colour that humans cannot see? We cannot even imagine this because we have to use our visual brain to imagine with and it lacks any representation of ultraviolet colours.

Insects, meanwhile, have compound eyes with thousands of separate lenses rather than a single eye like birds and mammals. They too can see in the ultraviolet. Lots of insects have an acute sense of smell, using scented trails to lead others to food; or communicating with each other using pheromones that they can detect through their antennae. What is their experience like? What is it like to smell a rotting mouse corpse using a sensitive antenna? For a fly that lays her eggs in such a corpse, it presumably smells delightful. From learning about the senses of other animals we must conclude that, in this forest, every creature would be having a completely different experience. They would each inhabit an entirely different world, or *Umwelt*.

We may still be tempted to ask which animals are conscious at all. On the one hand, consciousness could be an all-or-nothing phenomenon, with some creatures having it and others not.

Descartes believed that only humans had souls, and other animals were 'unfeeling automata'. On the other hand, consciousness might be a continuous variable, with some having more than others. Any viable theory of consciousness ought to specify which creatures are conscious, in what way, and why.

How can we find the answer? We hit again that curious feature of consciousness that we cannot know; there is no consciousness-detecting machine; no inner sanctum of consciousness production in the brain that we might find in some animals and not others. So the question remains unanswerable, and if a question is unanswerable it may be best to stop asking it and ask instead why we are so confused.

Yet this one will not go away, if for no other reason than that we care about animal suffering. An unconscious automaton cannot suffer. So if Descartes and his successors are right, then we need not worry about animal pain. Yet animals appear obviously capable of suffering. A cat with thick, shiny fur, bright eyes, and in a playful mood, seems obviously happy; a cat with thin, bedraggled fur, dull eyes, limping from an infected gash on its leg seems obviously to be in pain. Yet can we be sure our intuitions are correct?

No, we cannot. From childhood we tend to adopt the intentional stance towards anything that moves in a purposeful way. We attribute agency to even the simplest robot using what is sometimes called our *hyperactive agency detection device*. We can happily interact in natural, emotional ways with humanoid robot heads covered with elastic skin that are able to change facial expressions. And many of us attribute more feelings to animals that are soft and cuddly and look like us, such as cats and rabbits with their forward-looking eyes, than to scaly or slimy creatures. So, we cannot trust these intuitions.

To break through this impasse, biologist Marian Stamp Dawkins argued that if an animal is really suffering it should be willing to work to avoid the cause of its distress. Concerned about battery hens provided with no litter to scratch in, she devised an experiment in which they had to push aside a heavy curtain to reach a cage with litter. Although they clearly preferred the cage with litter, they would not make much effort to get there. Behavioural measures like this can help us gauge the extent of animals' suffering, but may still leave some people saying, 'Yes, but is it just behaving as though it hurts or is it *really* feeling the pain?'

The best way to answer this would be to have a theory about just what abilities and behaviours imply consciousness and which do not; and, in the case of animal consciousness, there are several such theories.

Mirrors, selves, and other minds

Look in a mirror and what do you see? Yourself of course. This seems trivial to us because of our highly social brains, but in fact it is quite an accomplishment. It means you must have a sense of self, which is why mirror self-recognition has become such a well-known test. If being conscious relies on having a sense of self, as some people argue, then we need to find out which animals can recognize themselves in a mirror.

As any pet owner will attest, cats, dogs, and rabbits cannot. On first seeing a mirror, they may rush up to it with interest, and even look around the back for the other dog or rabbit they can see, but they soon get bored. Some fish will fight their own reflections, and some birds display to them. They obviously assume that they are seeing another fish or bird. But what about monkeys and apes?

In 1872, Charles Darwin (1809–82) gave a mirror to two young orang-utans in London zoo, describing how they played in front of it and tried to kiss their reflections, but he could not be sure that they recognized themselves. Over a century later, psychologist

24. Mirror self-recognition is used as a test for self-awareness. In Gallup's experiments chimpanzees tried to rub off a spot seen only in the mirror.

Gordon Gallup devised a test to find out (Figure 24). He let a group of young chimpanzees play with mirrors, then he anaesthetized them and painted two obvious red spots above one eye and the opposite ear. When they awoke, he let them look in the mirror. You or I, in such a situation, would immediately see the marks and probably try to touch them or rub them off. So did the chimpanzees. They touched the spots more often than they touched the same place on the opposite side of their face.

Human children pass this same test from about 18 months onwards. Of the other great apes, chimpanzees, bonobos, and orang-utans mostly do too, but gorillas do not. Tests with monkeys have shown no self-recognition, even though they can use mirrors in other ways, such as to reach things they can see only in a reflection. This suggests a great divide between the great apes and the rest, but there are many doubts and problems. For example, for some monkeys, eye contact is threatening, preventing them from looking at their reflection. Birds have differently organized brains from humans, and they mostly fail the test—although one magpie has been filmed excitedly trying to remove a spot. Whales and dolphins are extremely intelligent and may well have a concept of self, but having no hands with which to touch a spot, their ability has to be inferred from the way they play with and use mirrors. This test, interesting as it is, provides no firm answers about consciousness. Gallup, who devised it, is convinced that chimpanzees not only recognize themselves in mirrors but have a concept of self, a notion of a personal past and future, and self-awareness. Sceptics agree only that chimpanzees can use their reflection to inspect their body and argue that this does not imply self-awareness.

Another way of getting at self-awareness is to investigate whether different species can appreciate that other individuals have minds. If an animal has a 'theory of mind', as humans do, then maybe it can turn that understanding inwards and see itself as having desires, intentions, and feelings. Deception is relevant here because, to deceive someone else, you have to imagine what they know or want. Chimpanzees have been seen distracting others while they grab food, or hiding behind rocks to indulge in illicit sex, but some clever experiments by primatologist Daniel Povinelli cast doubt on their social insight.

Knowing that chimpanzees naturally beg for food from humans and from each other, Povinelli designed an experiment in which two experimenters offered food to them. One experimenter had a blindfold over her eyes and the other over her mouth but this made no difference; the chimpanzees begged equally to both, and even (in a different experiment) to an experimenter with a bucket over her head. It seems they have no idea that it is pointless to beg from someone who cannot see you. The consensus for now is that chimpanzees do understand others' goals and intentions, but do not have a theory of mind. But even this is uncertain, and the implications for animal consciousness are more uncertain still.

One final dividing line is language. Many animals have rich forms of communication but not true language. For example, vervet monkeys make at least three different alarm calls to warn others about different kinds of danger; bees perform elaborate dances to communicate information about food sources and distances; and male birds inform others of their impressive status by the length and variety of their songs. These ways of communicating are critical to animals' lives, but these signals have fixed meanings and cannot be recombined to make new ones. In true language, arbitrary sounds or signs are combined in a potentially infinite number of ways to produce an equally vast number of possible meanings. These combinations are new memes that can be copied from one person to another.

Attempts to teach language to other species have almost completely failed, despite some early hopes of success. There are several chimpanzees, gorillas, and orang-utans who have learned American sign language, and some have vocabularies of several hundred signs. A gorilla called Koko even passed the mirror recognition test, suggesting that her training with sign language had had other effects too; but mostly these apes use their signs to ask for food. They do not spontaneously name things, play with words, or tell everyone what they are up to, as young children do.

The relevance to consciousness is this. Some people argue that the addition of language completely transforms minds, bringing about the essentials of consciousness, including the sense of self, theory of mind, and the ability to think about past and future. In other words, without language no animal can be conscious, and since there is little or no evidence for language in other species we alone must be conscious. But how can we tell? If this problem seems difficult, it is nothing compared to the confusions surrounding the question of how, when, and why consciousness evolved in the first place.

The function of consciousness

Why are we conscious at all? You might argue that since we *are* conscious, consciousness itself must have had an evolutionary function.

At first sight this argument seems eminently plausible. The theory of evolution by natural selection is one of the great insights of science—simple, yet extraordinarily powerful. Some say it is the best idea anybody ever had. As Darwin realized, a simple reiterative process can create the most intricate and functional designs apparently out of nowhere. It works like this—start with something; make lots of copies of it with slight variations; select just one of these; and then repeat the process. That's all.

The power lies with the effect of selection. Darwin began by explaining artificial selection, in which people choose to breed from some animals and not others and in this way to increase desirable characteristics, but he realized that the same process must operate with the blind processes of natural selection. That is, in a world with insufficient food, space, light, and air to go round, inevitably some creatures will do better than others, and whatever it was that helped them in the competition for survival will be passed on to their offspring, and so the process continues. As it does so, characteristics such as eyes, wings, hair, and teeth all appear and evolve. These are the adaptations that helped the animals to survive, and will be passed on if they breed.

Is consciousness an adaptation? It might seem that it must be, because maladaptive characteristics are soon weeded out by selection, but there are two other main possibilities: consciousness might be a useless by-product, or it might be an inseparable component of something else that is adaptive (even if it does not appear to be). There are theories of consciousness of all three types but, as we shall see, they all land us in trouble.

Let's begin with what seems to be a perfectly natural idea—that humans might have evolved without consciousness. In other words, consciousness was an optional extra, and we might all have been zombies. 'Why not?' the argument goes. 'I can perfectly well imagine a world in which people look and behave exactly the same but inside there is no awareness; no "what it is like" to be me.' This intuition has fuelled thought experiments involving zombie twins, and even a complete zombie Earth. But there is a serious problem.

Imagine a replay of evolution in which some of our ancestors were zombies while others were conscious—we can call them *conscies*. Natural selection now gets to work on this mixed population of zombies and conscies, and what happens? Absolutely nothing happens because, *by definition*, zombies are indistinguishable from conscies. They look the same, act the same, and say the same kinds of things. This means that natural selection would have nothing to work on. Any increase or decrease in zombies over conscies would be entirely random. This curious conclusion makes nonsense of the idea that consciousness is an optional extra, a useless by-product, or an epiphenomenon. It is best to throw out the whole idea of zombies and move on.

This leaves two other possibilities: either consciousness is an adaptation or it necessarily comes along with, or is an aspect of, other adaptations.

If consciousness is an adaptation, if *subjective experience* is adaptive in its own right, it makes sense to say that we might have evolved without it. But in this case we would not be philosophers' zombies; we would be more like Hollywood Haitian zombies—creatures deficient in something important. Evolution would then have favoured the conscies. If you take this view, you have to explain what consciousness adds, and you will remember the trouble we had with the concept of consciousness actually doing anything. For a start, it is difficult to see how subjective experiences or *what it's like to be* could actually affect anything. Then there is all the evidence that conscious experiences come too late to be the cause of actions or to have the kinds of effects they are commonly thought to have.

Nevertheless, there are several theories of this kind. Baars claims that the theatre metaphor is useful and consciousness is 'a major biological adaptation'. Dehaene claims consciousness is useful for sharing information. Biologist Jon Mallatt and neurologist Todd Feinberg claim that consciousness evolved 520 million years ago to direct animals' behaviour. Psychologist Nicholas Humphrey proposes that consciousness evolved for social functions, giving our ancestors an 'inner eye' so they could use introspection to predict the actions of others and to form complex alliances and relationships. In a later version he argues that evolving brains being constantly turned in on themselves has led to the 'magical-mystery show' inside our heads whose function is to motivate our lives.

Yet with all these theories we must still ask why 'what it's like' (i.e. subjective experience) provides a selective advantage over and above the specific abilities that have evolved. The final possibility is to throw out the idea that *experiences themselves* can do anything. In this 'illusionist' view consciousness is not an adaptation but an illusion, not because it is a useless by-product, but because it is not something separable from intelligence, perception, thinking, self-concept, language, or internal modelling.

One example is neuroscientist Michael Graziano's *attention schema theory*. This suggests that attention evolved from a simple alerting device into a complex system that allows us to deliberately and internally direct our attention. We then model this internal or *covert* attention to create an attention schema or *semi-magical self-description* that feels like 'something tangible inside me'. The point is that this model of an inner self, although useful, is wrong.

Metzinger's 'phenomenal self-models' are adaptive but the self they describe cannot be because it does not exist. Douglas Hofstadter is famous for playing with recursive, self-referential loops and in *I am a strange loop* describes the self as one of these loops, and free will and consciousness as illusions. In any such theory the loops, models, and representations have functions and are adaptive but there is no extra adaptation called 'consciousness' as well.

Conscious machines?

Could computers ever be conscious? This has been another thorny question with a long and tangled history. Some argue that only living things can be conscious, while others claim that it is the functions the computer carries out that are relevant, not what it is made of. On the delusionist theory of consciousness the answer is simple. If any machine had language or memes or whatever it takes to be able to ask the question, 'Am I conscious now?', and concoct theories about its inner self and its own mind, then it would be as deluded as we are and think it was conscious in the same deluded way. Otherwise it would, like non-human animals, construct temporary perceptual worlds through its interactions with the environment, but never imagine it was experiencing them.

Could the Internet or cyberspace be conscious? The idea of a 'global brain' has a long history but it is becoming ever more plausible with the increasing speed, volume, and interconnectedness of information. Since our own consciousness depends on a hyper-connected nervous system it may not be impossible for this vast artificial system also to model itself and ask difficult questions about its own experiences (Box 8).

Delusionism

The confusion we have reached is deep and serious, and I suspect reveals fundamental flaws in the way we think about consciousness.

Box 8 Memes

Memes are habits, skills, behaviours, or stories that are copied from person to person by imitation. Like genes, memes compete to be copied, but instead of being chemicals locked inside cells, they are information that jumps from brain to brain; or from brains to computers, books, and works of art. The winning memes spread across the world, shaping our minds and cultures as they go. The rest die out.

Memes club together to make vast *memeplexes*. Many of these enhance our lives, such as financial systems, scientific theories, legal systems, sports, and the arts. But others are more like infections or parasites that jump from host to host, including quack remedies, cults, conspiracy theories, chain letters, computer viruses, and malware. Their basic structure is a 'copy-me' instruction backed up with threats and promises.

Many religions are like this, which is why Richard Dawkins calls them 'viruses of the mind'. Roman Catholics must have lots of children and pass on the memes of their own indoctrination, relying on faith and the suppression of doubts. Praying, singing hymns, going to church, and contributing to impressive buildings are costly behaviours that benefit these memes, and are encouraged with untestable threats of everlasting hell and promises of heaven. Islam protects its memes by prescribing severe punishment for unbelievers and even worse for apostates who abandon their faith. Religions' memes can therefore replicate successfully even if they are untrue or even harmful. At the extreme, religious memes kill their carriers, as martyrs who die for their faith.

But what about consciousness? One idea is that the self is itself a memeplex: a group of memes that thrive together and is strengthened every time the word 'I' is used. Phrases such as 'I want...', 'I believe...', and 'I know...' all fuel the illusion of a persistent inner self who has conscious experiences. But really there are just words being copied and memes competing with each other to make us who we are—deluded meme machines.

Could our misunderstandings be so bad that we need to throw out some basic assumptions and start all over again?

My own view is this. Consciousness is an illusion: an enticing and compelling illusion that lures us into believing that our minds are separate from our bodies; that consciousness is a stream or theatre; that some experiences are 'in consciousness' and others 'outside consciousness'; that some brain processes are conscious while others are unconscious. The underlying belief is that if you ask, 'What is in Sue's consciousness now?', there must be a correct answer, because some of her thoughts and perceptions are conscious and the rest are not. Making these assumptions has, I suggest, led the field of consciousness studies into asking the wrong questions and getting bogged down in useless arguments. Instead of asking how consciousness 'arises', 'emerges from', or is 'produced by' the brain we should be asking why we have got it so wrong.

The reason we are so confused, I suggest, is this. Take the simple question, 'Am I conscious now?'. Whenever I ask this question (I expect you are asking it now), the answer is 'Yes'. So it is easy and natural to assume that this is always the case as long as I am awake. But what about when I am not asking the question? The situation is reminiscent of change blindness and grand illusion theory. With vision, every time you look, you see a rich visual world, so you falsely assume it is always there. It is like trying to open the fridge quickly enough to see if the light is always on or, as William James put it in 1890, 'trying to turn up the gas quickly enough to see how the darkness looks' (Figure 25). You cannot use light to see what darkness is like.

This, I suggest, is how the grand delusion of consciousness comes about. It arises because we clever, thinking, talking humans can ask ourselves such questions as, 'Am I conscious now?' or 'What am I conscious of?'. When we do so, an answer is instantly concocted, and in that moment a 'now', a 'stream of experiences', and an

25. What is it like when you are not asking the question, 'Am I conscious now?'. Trying to find out is like trying to open the fridge door quickly enough to see whether the light is always on.

'experiencing self' all appear together; a moment later they are gone. Next time we ask, a new self and a new stream are concocted. So we (wrongly) assume that they are continuously present.

Observing more closely we notice that something changes when we ask this question. We seem to become more conscious just by

asking about consciousness. So this prompts another question—
'What was I conscious of a moment ago?'. Once again we get
an answer, this time based on what we can remember from a
moment before. Indeed whenever we ask such questions we
get an answer. So we jump to the false conclusion that at every
waking moment we must be a conscious self, experiencing a
stream of conscious experiences—because whenever we asked,
we found it was true. The rest follows from there. If we go on to
believe that we are always conscious, and construct metaphors
about streams and theatres, we only dig ourselves deeper and
deeper into confusion.

The truth is that consciousness is an attribution we make. We call
some of our thoughts, perceptions, and actions 'conscious' and
others 'unconscious', but this distinction is based only on them
being accessible when we ask about them. When we are not asking
the question, there are no contents of consciousness and no
experiencer. Instead, the brain carries on doing multiple things
in parallel—as in Dennett's multiple drafts theory—and none is
either in consciousness or out of it. In this new way of thinking
about consciousness many old problems disappear. We do not
need to explain how consciousness is produced by, or emerges
from, the objective activity of the brain, because it does not. We do
not have to explain the magic difference between brain activity
which is conscious and that which is not, because there is no
difference. We do not have to wonder how subjective experiences
evolved and whether they have a function of their own because
they do not. There is no stream of experiences—only fleeting
events that give rise to a false impression.

If this is true, only creatures capable of being so deluded could be
conscious in the way we are. This may mean that humans are
unique among animals because only we have language and theory
of mind, and we alone model ourselves as having an inner self.
Other animals go about their lives creating passing perceptual

worlds as they go—creating experiences, if you like, but not streams of consciousness experienced by a self.

Perhaps there is something it is like to be each fleeting construction: the tangled branches rushing past as a bird lands on its perch; the pain of stretched muscles as a horse gallops or a rabbit leaps to safety; the feel of closing in on that insect as the bat's sonar guides its flight. If so, these are free-floating experiences that come and go, and are not had by anyone. So there is no true answer to the question 'What is it like to be a bat?', any more than there is anything it is like to be us most of the time. There is only an answer when we construct a model of self or ask the question and, as far as we know, bats don't do that.

Can we escape from delusion? I believe we can. Many people claim that insight comes through long practice of meditation and mindfulness, and neuroscientists are studying how these methods for training the attention change the brain. Zen koans include exactly the sort of questions that are relevant here: 'Who am I?' 'When is now?' 'What is this?'. I have spent a long time sitting with these questions and finding that the ordinary sense of being a self having a stream of experiences disappears. Mindfulness entails staying alert, open, and fully present in the moment, whether meditating or not. This apparently simple technique can, with long practice, give rise to a state in which phenomena arise and fall away but without any sense of time or place, and with no one experiencing them. The dualism between 'me' and 'the world' disappears into non-duality.

If all this is so we should not be hunting for the mythical 'neural correlates of consciousness', but rather for the correlates of processes that create the illusions in the first place, and of those states in which such illusions disappear. My hope is that one day our scientific understanding of consciousness will come together with personal insight. There are already some scientists with deep personal practice, and practitioners who study the science, holding out the hope that first- and third-person perspectives will eventually come together and let us see clearly. Both intellectually and in our own experience we should be able to stop being deluded and see through all those illusions of self, free will, and consciousness.

Further reading

General books

All the topics in this book are covered in more detail in S. J. Blackmore, *Consciousness: An Introduction* (London: Hodder & Stoughton, 2010; New York: Oxford University Press, 2011), along with exercises, demonstrations, and an extensive list of references.

For encyclopaedic coverage, see *The Blackwell Companion to Consciousness* edited by M. Velmans (Oxford: Blackwell, 2007) or the *Cambridge Handbook of Consciousness* edited by P. D. Zelazo, M. Moscovitch, and E. Thompson (Cambridge: Cambridge University Press, 2007).

William James's two-volume classic is *The Principles of Psychology* (London: MacMillan, 1890).

Daniel Dennett's books provide a deep and fascinating philosophical and evolutionary approach, especially *Consciousness Explained* (Boston, MA: Little, Brown and Co., 1991) and *From Bacteria to Bach and Back* (London: Allen Lane, 2017).

For opposing views, see D. Chalmers, *The Character of Consciousness* (Oxford: Oxford University Press, 2010); and J. Searle, *The Mystery of Consciousness* (London: Granta Books, 1998).

And for some fun reading, try D. R. Hofstadter and D. C. Dennett (eds), *The Mind's I: Fantasies and Reflections on Self and Soul* (London: Penguin, 1981).

For psychology and neuroscience, try F. Crick, *The Astonishing Hypothesis* (New York: Scribner's, 1994) (a strong reductionist view); G. M. Edelman and G. Tononi, *Consciousness: How Matter Becomes Imagination* (London: Penguin, 2000); C. Koch,

Consciousness: Confessions of a Romantic Reductionist
(Cambridge, MA: MIT Press, 2012); and S. Dehaene,
*Consciousness and the Brain: Deciphering How the Brain
Codes Our Thoughts* (London: Penguin, 2014).

Journals and web resources

The main journals are the *Journal of Consciousness Studies* and
Consciousness and Cognition, both print and online; and the new
open-access journal, *Neuroscience of Consciousness*. Other online
journals include *Psyche: An Interdisciplinary Journal of Research
on Consciousness* and *Science and Consciousness Review*. For an
excellent source of many classic and contemporary papers, all
available in full, see *Online Papers on Consciousness*, provided by
David Chalmers at: <http://consc.net/online>.

For authoritative articles on philosophy, see the *Stanford
Encyclopedia of Philosophy* at: <https://plato.stanford.edu/>.

My website provides other links and online articles at: <http://
www.susanblackmore.uk/>.

Chapter 1: Why the mystery?

For readings on the hard problem, see J. Shear (ed.), *Explaining
Consciousness—The 'Hard Problem'* (Cambridge, MA: MIT Press,
1997).

And, more generally on philosophy of mind, D. Chalmers (ed.),
Philosophy of Mind: Classical and Contemporary Readings
(Oxford: Oxford University Press, 2002).

Nagel's original paper on the bat is T. Nagel, 'What is it like to be a
bat?', *Philosophical Review* (1974), 83: 435–50.

It is widely reprinted, including in Chalmers's anthology, *Philosophy of
Mind: Classical and Contemporary Readings* (Oxford: Oxford
University Press, 2002), where you can also find Block's paper
'Some concepts of consciousness' and Dennett's, 'Quining qualia'.

Zombies are discussed in D. Chalmers, *The Conscious Mind* (Oxford:
Oxford University Press, 1996) and *The Stanford Encyclopedia of
Philosophy*, with the *Journal of Consciousness Studies* (1995), 2(4),
devoting a special issue to the subject.

For Cartesian theatre and Cartesian materialism, see D. C. Dennett,
Consciousness Explained (Boston, MA: Little, Brown and Co., 1991).

Chapter 2: The human brain

For readings on NCCs, see T. Metzinger (ed.), *Neural Correlates of Consciousness* (Cambridge, MA: MIT Press, 2000).

Or, for a more technical update, C. Koch, M. Massimini, M. Boly, and G. Tononi, 'Neural correlates of consciousness: progress and problems', *Nature Reviews Neuroscience* (2016), 17(5): 307–21.

For vision and blindsight, see A. D. Milner and M. A. Goodale, *The Visual Brain in Action* (Oxford: Oxford University Press, 1995); and L. Weiskrantz, *Blindsight* (Oxford University Press, 2009).

For different views on neuropsychology, see V. S. Ramachandran and S. Blakeslee, *Phantoms in the Brain* (London: Fourth Estate, 1998); C. Koch, *Consciousness: Confessions of a Romantic Reductionist* (Cambridge, MA: MIT Press, 2012); and S. Dehaene *Consciousness and the Brain* (New York: Viking, 2014).

For synaesthesia, see R. E. Cytowic and D. M. Eagleman, *Wednesday is Indigo Blue: Discovering the Brain of Synesthesia* (Cambridge, MA: MIT Press, 2009).

Chapter 3: Time and space

Libet's delay is discussed in most general books on consciousness and in his own book, B. Libet, *Mind Time: The Temporal Factor in Consciousness* (Cambridge, MA: Harvard University Press, 2004).

Critical discussions of timing, the cutaneous rabbit, and other experiments are in D. C. Dennett, *Consciousness Explained* (Boston, MA: Little, Brown and Co., 1991).

Global workspace theory originated with B. J. Baars, *A Cognitive Theory of Consciousness* (Cambridge: Cambridge University Press, 1988).

Neuronal GWT is described in S. Dehaene, *Consciousness and the Brain* (New York: Viking, 2014).

For other theories, see G. M. Edelman, *Wider than the Sky: The Phenomenal Gift of Consciousness* (London: Allen Lane, 2004); R. Penrose, *Shadows of the Mind* (Oxford: Oxford University Press, 1994); and (for an overview) W. Seager, *Theories of Consciousness* (London: Routledge, 2016).

Chapter 4: A grand illusion

For embodied and enactive cognition, see A. Clark, *Supersizing the Mind: Embodiment, Action, and Cognitive Extension* (Cambridge:

Cambridge University Press, 2008); and L. Shapiro, *The Routledge Handbook of Embodied Cognition* (London: Routledge, 2014).

For the importance of emotions, see A. Damasio, *The Feeling of What Happens: Body, Emotion and the Making of Consciousness* (London: Heinemann, 2000).

And for two types of processing, D. Kahneman, *Thinking, Fast and Slow* (London: Macmillan, 2011).

For filling-in, see V. S. Ramachandran and S. Blakeslee, *Phantoms in the Brain* (London: Fourth Estate, 1998); and H. Komatsu, 'The neural mechanisms of perceptual filling-in', *Nature Reviews Neuroscience* (2006), 7(3): 220–31.

For grand illusion theory, try A. Mack and I. Rock, *Inattentional Blindness* (Cambridge, MA: MIT Press, 1998); A. Noë (ed.), *Is the Visual World a Grand Illusion?* (Thorverton: Imprint Academic, 2002); and a special issue of the *Journal of Consciousness Studies* (2016), vol. 23, on illusionist theories of consciousness, edited by K. Frankish.

Chapter 5: The self

For a simple introduction to ego and bundle theories as well as the teletransporter thought experiment, see D. Parfit, 'Divided minds and the nature of persons', in S. Schneider (ed.), *Science Fiction and Philosophy: From Time Travel to Superintelligence* (London: Wiley-Blackwell, 2016), pp. 91–8.

Opposing views on self are aired in a special issue of the *Journal of Consciousness Studies* reprinted as S. Gallagher and J. Shear (eds), *Models of the Self* (Thorverton: Imprint Academic, 1999).

Split brain cases are described in M. S. Gazzaniga, *Nature's Mind* (London: Basic Books, 1992).

And dissociation in E. R. Hilgard, *Divided Consciousness: Multiple Controls in Human Thought and Action* (New York: Wiley, 1986).

Early cases, and James's own theory of self, are in W. James, *The Principles of Psychology* (London: MacMillan, 1890).

Good introductions to Buddhism are S. Batchelor, *Buddhism Without Beliefs: A Contemporary Guide to Awakening* (London: Bloomsbury, 1997); and W. Rahula, *What the Buddha Taught* (London: Gordon Fraser; New York: Grove Press, 1959).

For books on self, see S. Harris, *Waking Up: A Guide to Spirituality without Religion* (London: Simon & Schuster, 2014); T. Metzinger,

The Ego Tunnel: The Science of the Mind and the Myth of the Self
(London: Basic Books, 2009); B. Hood, *The Self Illusion* (Oxford:
Oxford University Press, 2012); and A. Damasio, *Self Comes to Mind:
Constructing the Conscious Brain* (London: Heinemann, 2010).

Chapter 6: Conscious will

For the debate on Libet's experiment, see B. Libet, 'Unconscious
cerebral initiative and the role of conscious will in voluntary
action', *The Behavioral and Brain Sciences* (1985), 8: 529–39 (with
commentaries in the same issue, pp. 539–66); and 10: 318–21. The
experiment is widely discussed, but most critically in D. C. Dennett,
Consciousness Explained (Boston, MA: Little, Brown and Co., 1991).
The first table tipping experiment is by M. Faraday, 'Experimental
investigations of table moving', *The Athenaeum* (1853), 1340: 801–3.
For further examples and Wegner's theory, see D. M. Wegner, *The
Illusion of Conscious Will* (Cambridge, MA: MIT Press, 2002).
For opposing views, see S. Harris, *Free Will* (New York: Free Press,
2012); and M. S. Gazzaniga, *Who's in Charge: Free Will and the
Science of the Brain* (London: Robinson, 2016).
And for my interviews, S. Blackmore, *Conversations on Consciousness*
(Oxford: Oxford University Press, 2005).

Chapter 7: Altered states of consciousness

Overviews of the topics discussed here can be found in J. A. Hobson,
Dreaming: An Introduction to the Science of Sleep (New York:
Oxford University Press, 2002); D. Nutt, *Drugs—Without the Hot
Air: Minimising the Harms of Legal and Illegal Drugs*
(Cambridge: UIT, 2012); M. Jay, *High Society* (London: Thames
and Hudson, 2013); and M. Earleywine, *Understanding
Marijuana: A New Look at the Scientific Evidence* (New York:
Oxford University Press, 2002).
For OBEs and NDEs, see S. Blackmore, *Seeing Myself: The New
Science of Out-of-Body Experiences* (London: Robinson, 2017).
For a practical guide to meditation, see M. Batchelor, *Meditation for
Life* (London: Frances Lincoln, 2001).
And for related neuroscience, R. Hanson, *Buddha's Brain: The
Practical Neuroscience of Happiness, Love and Wisdom* (Oakland,
CA: New Harbinger, 2009); and E. Thompson, *Waking,*

Dreaming, Being: Self and Consciousness in Neuroscience, Meditation, and Philosophy (New York: Columbia University Press, 2014).

My struggles with koans are in S. Blackmore, *Zen and the Art of Consciousness* (Oxford: Oneworld, 2011).

Chapter 8: The evolution of consciousness

The evolution of consciousness is discussed in most general books on consciousness and in N. Humphrey, *A History of the Mind* (London: Chatto & Windus, 1992); T. E. Feinberg and J. M. Mallatt, *The Ancient Origins of Consciousness: How the Brain Created Experience* (Cambridge, MA: MIT Press, 2016); and D. C. Dennett *From Bacteria to Bach and Back: The Evolution of Minds* (London: Allen Lane, 2017).

For specific theories, see N. Humphrey, *Soul Dust: The Magic of Consciousness* (Princeton, NJ: Princeton University Press, 2011); M. Graziano, *Consciousness and the Social Brain* (Oxford: Oxford University Press, 2013); T. Metzinger, *The Ego Tunnel* (New York: Basic Books, 2009); and D. Hofstadter, *I am a Strange Loop* (New York: Basic Books, 2007).

Research on animal minds is reviewed in M. S. Dawkins, *Why Animals Matter: Animal Consciousness, Animal Welfare, and Human Well-being* (Oxford: Oxford University Press, 2012); and see also S. Montgomery, *The Soul of an Octopus: A Surprising Exploration into the Wonder of Consciousness* (London: Simon & Schuster, 2015).

For memes, see R. A. Aunger (ed.), *Darwinizing Culture: The Status of Memetics as a Science* (Oxford: Oxford University Press, 2000); and S. Blackmore, *The Meme Machine* (Oxford: Oxford University Press, 1999).

Index

E

D

Consciousness

SOCIAL MEDIA
Very Short Introduction

Join our community

www.oup.com/vsi

- Join us online at the official Very Short Introductions **Facebook** page.
- Access the thoughts and musings of our authors with our online **blog**.
- Sign up for our monthly **e-newsletter** to receive information on all new titles publishing that month.
- Browse the full range of Very Short Introductions online.
- Read **extracts** from the Introductions for free.
- If you are a teacher or lecturer you can order inspection copies quickly and simply via our website.

ONLINE CATALOGUE
A Very Short Introduction

Our online catalogue is designed to make it easy to find your ideal Very Short Introduction. View the entire collection by subject area, watch author videos, read sample chapters, and download reading guides.

http://global.oup.com/uk/academic/general/vsi_list/

AUTISM
A Very Short Introduction
Uta Frith

This *Very Short Introduction* offers a clear statement on what is currently known about autism and Asperger syndrome. Explaining the vast array of different conditions that hide behind these two labels, and looking at symptoms from the full spectrum of autistic disorders, it explores the possible causes for the apparent rise in autism and also evaluates the links with neuroscience, psychology, brain development, genetics, and environmental causes including MMR and Thimerosal. This short, authoritative, and accessible book also explores the psychology behind social impairment and savantism and sheds light on what it is like to live inside the mind of the sufferer.

CONSCIENCE
A VERY SHORT
INTRODUCTION

Paul Strohm

In the West conscience has been relied upon for two thousand years as a judgement that distinguishes right from wrong. It has effortlessly moved through every period division and timeline between the ancient, medieval, and modern. The Romans identified it, the early Christians appropriated it, and Reformation Protestants and loyal Catholics relied upon its advice and admonition. Today it is embraced with equal conviction by non-religious and religious alike. Considering its deep historical roots and exploring what it has meant to successive generations, Paul Strohm highlights why this particularly European concept deserves its reputation as 'one of the prouder Western contributions to human rights and human dignity throughout the world.

www.oup.com/vsi

FREE SPEECH
A Very Short Introduction
Nigel Warburton

'I disapprove of what you say, but I will defend to the death your right to say it' This slogan, attributed to Voltaire, is frequently quoted by defenders of free speech. Yet it is rare to find anyone prepared to defend all expression in every circumstance, especially if the views expressed incite violence. So where do the limits lie? What is the real value of free speech? Here, Nigel Warburton offers a concise guide to important questions facing modern society about the value and limits of free speech: Where should a civilized society draw the line? Should we be free to offend other people's religion? Are there good grounds for censoring pornography? Has the Internet changed everything? This Very Short Introduction is a thought-provoking, accessible, and up-to-date examination of the liberal assumption that free speech is worth preserving at any cost.

'The genius of Nigel Warburton's *Free Speech* lies not only in its extraordinary clarity and incisiveness. Just as important is the way Warburton addresses freedom of speech - and attempts to stifle it - as an issue for the 21st century. More than ever, we need this book.'

Denis Dutton, University of Canterbury, New Zealand

www.oup.com/vsi

Memory
A Very Short Introduction
Michael J. Benton

Why do we remember events from our childhood as if they happened yesterday, but not what we did last week? Why does our memory seem to work well sometimes and not others? What happens when it goes wrong? Can memory be improved or manipulated, by psychological techniques or even 'brain implants'? How does memory grow and change as we age? And what of so-called 'recovered' memories? This book brings together the latest research in neuroscience and psychology, and weaves in case-studies, anecdotes, and even literature and philosophy, to address these and many other important questions about the science of memory - how it works, and why we can't live without it.

www.oup.com/vsi